The State of Religion & Young People 2020
RELATIONAL AUTHORITY

Springtide™
RESEARCH INSTITUTE

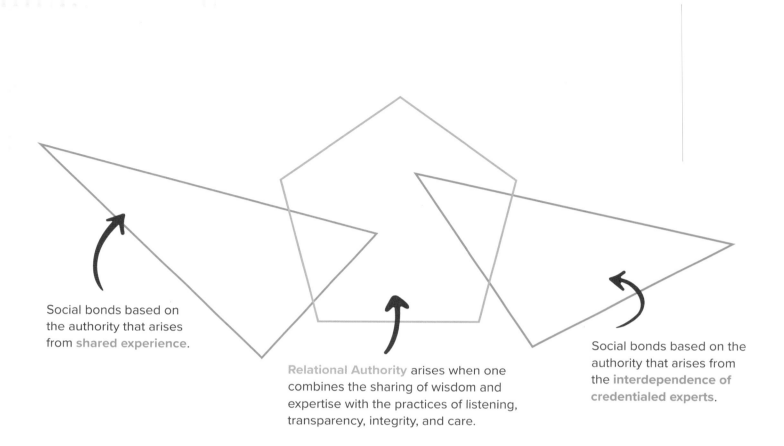

Social bonds based on the authority that arises from **shared experience**.

Relational Authority arises when one combines the sharing of wisdom and expertise with the practices of listening, transparency, integrity, and care.

Social bonds based on the authority that arises from the **interdependence of credentialed experts**.

A note about the cover:

The cover symbolizes various connections that hold society together. The blue triangle represents social bonds based on what people have in common and the authority that arises from shared experience. The burnt orange triangle represents social bonds based on difference and the authority that arises from the interdependence of credentialed experts. The gold pentagon represents Relational Authority, a model of social connection that responds to the complexities of the state of religion and young people—a model that insists that shared experience and expertise are both needed to have lasting influence in the lives of young people. Relational Authority arises when one combines the sharing of wisdom and expertise with the practices of listening, transparency, integrity, and care.

Springtide
RESEARCH INSTITUTE

Mission

Compelled by the urgent desire to listen and attend to the lives of young people (ages 13–25), Springtide™ Research Institute is committed to understanding the distinct ways new generations experience and express community, identity, and meaning.

We exist at the intersection of religious and human experience in the lives of young people. And we're here to listen.

We combine quantitative and qualitative research to reflect and amplify the lived realities of young people as they navigate shifting social, cultural, and religious landscapes. Delivering fresh data and actionable insights, we equip those who care about young people to care better.

A Springtide Tribute.
A Promise. A Pledge.

 TO YOU

. . . who are young, full of wonder and possibility. You who are navigating some of life's most important questions and most tumultuous waters. You who are sometimes flourishing and sometimes floundering and oftentimes both. You who are at once being and becoming.

We dedicate our work to your thriving.

We dedicate ourselves to understanding your inner and outer lives.

 TO YOU

. . . who are fiercely devoted to young people. You who advocate for and walk alongside young people with steadiness. You who are unwavering amid the waves.

We offer our research as an aid to the role you already play.

We offer ourselves as allies in accompaniment.

 **AND TO**

. . . the waves that crash, the currents that bend and beckon, the dark depths, and the effervescent crests. To this all-important period of life: worthy of considered listening and faithful retelling, worthy of companionship, worthy of care.

We situate our work at this intersection of human and religious experience in the lives of young people: a space of ebb and flow, of calm and chaos, of clear and murky moments.

A space we are dedicated to exploring and engaging

 **WITH YOU.**

Contents

Special Features

Conclusion 108

Introduction

Springtide Research Institute listens to the stories of young people, ages 13–25, and amplifies their voices through quantitative and qualitative sociological research. **Our work exists at the intersection of religious and human experience. We strive to understand how young people make sense of an increasingly complex world, so that those who care about young people can be equipped to care better.**

In 2020, we asked questions at this intersection—questions about meaning, vocation, relationships, religion, friendships, education, community, politics, and more—to **over 10,000 young people** through quantitative surveys. We explored, unpacked, and deepened these questions by listening to over **150 young people's stories** in qualitative interviews.

These numbers make *The State of Religion & Young People 2020* the largest available data set of this demographic in the United States.

In 2020, we launched a podcast called *The Voices of Young People Podcast* to share how young people speak for themselves about the things we discover in our data. And to unpack what care for young people really looks like, we've produced videos and webinars with guest experts and practitioners. Throughout our blogs, books, and reports, we share stories and insights into young people's inner and outer lives coupled with actionable ideas for those who care about young people to put into practice. **Many of these resources are available, linked, or listed throughout this report for hearing, interacting with, and diving deeper into the story these data are telling.**

Religion, understood broadly, is a hallmark of our interest in young people's inner and outer lives. For Springtide, the term *religious* is not a reference to a particular creed, code, or system, but rather a term that captures and categorizes a wide array of diverse impulses, questions, and connections. These are the impulses that inspire young people to pursue community, identity, meaning, and connection. And we recognize that these impulses are increasingly finding expression in ways that may not seem overtly religious—that is, they are not connected directly to a specific tradition or institution. Instead, the desire for meaning may show up in careers, club sports, or creative hobbies. Young people find outlets for justice, faith, or purpose in politics, volunteering, nature, or close relationships.

While these impulses could be simply called *human* values, we understand them as religious because we are particularly interested in the ways they are expressed and exercised within systems. This interests us because we are sociologists, looking for trends in behaviors amid social, cultural, and religious shifts. Systems are just trends: they are patterns, repeated behaviors, that start to indicate different ways of being, believing, and becoming. And the systems and markers we've long relied on to gauge, measure, or express religious impulses are changing.

RESOURCES

All the resources referenced in numbered marginal notes throughout this report are compiled in a list both at the end of this book and at *springtideresearch.org /thestate2020*.

Diverse, rich, and complex, the religious lives of young people are anything but easily categorized or codified. And yet categories give us a starting point for exploration. *The State of Religion & Young People 2020* uses categories like "affiliated" and "unaffiliated," common for assessing the religious identities of young people, for an initial, partial snapshot of their inner and outer lives. But alongside formal questions of *identity*—questions like self-ascribed affiliation or sense of personal religiosity and/or spirituality—we also ask questions of religious *practices* (i.e., attendance at various services, prayerful practices or habits, and so on) and questions of religious *belief* (i.e., strengthening or weakening faith, concept of a higher power, and so on).

By looking at identity, practice, and belief, we move past simple interpretations or assertions about young people's inner and outer lives and start to see something more complex—and more accurate—emerge. And precisely *because* it's more complex, it's all the more important that young people have trusted adults in their lives that will listen to, care for, and guide them. To be an effective mentor in the life of a young person today—amid many complexities—a new framework is needed.

This report presents not only salient findings but also actionable insights. We call them *Tide-Turning Tips:* concrete practices and ideas for turning the tide on the experience of loneliness, anxiety, depression, or meaninglessness that plague young people today.

 The way to turn the tide is through relationships.

 The most effective relationships practice Relational Authority.

Part I of this report highlights the changing cultural landscape through big-picture observations and insights from Springtide data. We present these findings in a way relevant to religious leaders working with young people.

Part II unpacks these findings and offers a framework for how to have an impact in the lives of young people amid new social and religious circumstances. **We offer both empirical data and a framework for action for a reason: we recognize that data alone are not enough to spur action that responds to real needs.**

We offer a framework, driven by our empirical findings, that shifts and builds upon a century of insights from the social sciences, called Relational Authority. At Springtide, we know that the need for relationships and expertise as guiding forces in the lives of young people hasn't changed. But other, larger factors have. We know that cultural realities—as vast as pluralism or as immediately felt as political polarization—affect how and whether young people seek meaning, trust others, build community, or understand their own identities. These factors also change how we relate to, trust, and depend on one another. **For religious leaders, advocates, ministers, educators, and anyone else caring for the inner and outer lives of young people, this means young people need to feel cared for *before they can be receptive* to the influence of others in their lives.** This dynamic is at the heart of Relational Authority.

Part II not only presents Relational Authority as a framework but also unpacks its five dimensions: listening, transparency, integrity, care, and expertise. Combined with brief special features on young people's feelings about and connections to virtual environments (for things like learning or worship), politics, and careers, this report offers both a sweeping account of current circumstances and a detailed, action-oriented look at the state of religion and young people in 2020.

"2020 was the year that Relational Authority became the only real pathway to having a lasting influence in the lives of young people."

Dr. Josh Packard,
Springtide Executive
Director

A CLOSER LOOK

Throughout this report, you'll find five special features, called "A Closer Look," that dive deeper into current events, modes of solidarity, virtual environments, politics, and careers, and how these things impact young people today.

PART I

RELIGION & YOUNG PEOPLE 2020

INTRODUCTION TO PART I

Caring for Young People *Better*

The State of Religion & Young People 2020 names realities that you may already see, feel, and experience in your work with young people. Our goal is to equip and empower you to do something in light of these realities with up-to-date data and practical actions.

This report confirms and builds on what our report *Belonging: Reconnecting America's Loneliest Generation* made clear earlier this year: Young people are experiencing record loneliness. They have low levels of trust in most traditional institutions, and they are likely not responding to the efforts these institutions are making to connect with them. But they are—amid all these realities—seeking meaning, navigating questions of identity, and pursuing community. **And they need trusted adults to listen to, care for, and guide them.**

READ

Read *Belonging: Reconnecting America's Loneliest Generation* and learn more about the findings and insights from that report.

Of young people ages 13–25 with no adult mentors, 24% say they never feel their life has meaning and purpose. *But* for those with even just one adult mentor, this number drops to 6%.

Your work with and for young people is more important than ever, and your impact can't be left to old, ineffective models or outdated understandings of the social and religious landscape. With more than 25% of young people ages 13–25 telling us they have *one or fewer* adult mentors in their lives, the need is critical. **Your positive impact in the life of a young person can't be left to chance.** This is the heart of our mission at Springtide and the motivation for this report: to help those who care for young people to care *better.*

We hear from people just like you, who are working hard to help young people flourish in human and religious ways—in their work, relationships, and their sense of identity; in their goals, communities, and contributions to the world. We see and hear about ways this hard work is making a positive impact in the lives of young people as well as ways it is proving frustrating and less effective than perhaps it once was.

The world has shifted in both subtle and significant ways, yet many of the models that guide care for young people today are based in yesterday's realities. They don't account for shifting social, religious, or cultural forces. They are not responsive to ever-changing current events. They don't consider the complexities of young people's inner and outer lives.

It is no wonder these old models are not as effective for connecting with young people as they once were. Whether you notice young people drifting from religious communities, disconnecting from peer and adult relationships, or seeming to flounder amid the pressures of decision-making around identity, education, careers, or politics, it's clear: **New frameworks are needed to help young people flourish.**

24%

of young people with **no adult mentors never feel like their life has meaning and purpose.**

Just **one adult relationship** reduces that percentage to **6%**.

And the work you do—the ways you aid and support their flourishing—could not be more urgently needed. Young people today report record levels of loneliness. Nearly 70% of young people ages 13–25 report having three or fewer meaningful interactions per day. Nearly 40% say they feel they have no one to talk to and that no one really knows them well, at least sometimes. More than one in four young people say they have one or fewer adults in their lives they can turn to if they need to talk.

WATCH

Watch a short video of Dr. Josh Packard unpacking the emotional pain that loneliness causes.

69%
have **3 or fewer meaningful interactions** in a regular day.

NEARLY
40% • • •
say they feel they have **no one to talk to and that no one really knows them well,** at least sometimes.

MORE THAN 1 in 4
young people say they have one or fewer adults in their lives they can turn to if they need to talk.

Your presence, work, ministry, service to, and advocacy for young people is crucial. Whether you work in campus ministry or faith-based advocacy; whether you lead a church, mosque, temple, or synagogue; wherever you are and however you care for the inner and outer lives of young people, your work is too important to be left to old models and outdated frameworks. *The State of Religion & Young People 2020: Relational Authority* offers data to help us see the needs of young people more clearly, a framework for responding to those needs more effectively, and actions for putting that framework into practice easily and immediately.

"
> **A lot of the time I feel like I haven't really had a sense of belonging. I've moved around a lot and haven't had friendships that lasted that long.**
"

Ben, 20

The Big Picture

Young people in the United States today need stronger connections with more adults in order to thrive. Data from our March 2020 report on loneliness, confirmed here, make this clear. *Belonging: Reconnecting America's Loneliest Generation* revealed that adding just one trusted adult in the life of a young person dramatically decreases their sense of loneliness and isolation.

We've dug deeper into this need for relationships, both within and outside of traditional religious structures. We've learned that there is a direct correlation between the number of trusted adults in the life of a young person and that young person's sense of meaning and purpose.

Only 50% of young people who report having no mentors also say their life has meaning and purpose, whereas nearly 70% of those who have *at least one* mentor report that their life has meaning and purpose. This number jumps to 85% for those who have two to four mentors. Incredibly, more than nine out of ten (91%) young people who have five or more mentors in their life report that they sense their life has meaning. The correlation is undeniable.

Mentors Create Meaning and Purpose

Percentages of young people who say their life has meaning and purpose by number of mentors

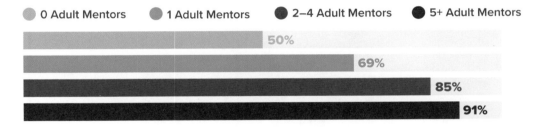

● 0 Adult Mentors ● 1 Adult Mentors ● 2–4 Adult Mentors ● 5+ Adult Mentors

- 50%
- 69%
- 85%
- 91%

But adults in the life of a young person aren't always *trusted* adults. And trusted adults aren't always effective at cultivating deep, meaningful relationships with lasting impact. The needs of young people that our data have uncovered suggest that the old frameworks and models aren't adequate. In light of new realities, we need new frameworks that will help us act differently.

To **act differently,** ▶▶▶ we need to **think differently.**

To **think differently,** ▶▶▶ we need to **look at the big picture.**

Surveying the Social, Religious & Cultural Landscape

Consider some of the broader social forces at work in the United States in the twenty-first century—factors that impact every second of our lives. These social forces, a few of which are listed here, are like the air we breathe: we're taking them in even though we're not conscious of doing so. **These forces impact two critical realities related to the state of religion and young people today: how young people form their religious identities and how we, as a society, are connected to one another.**

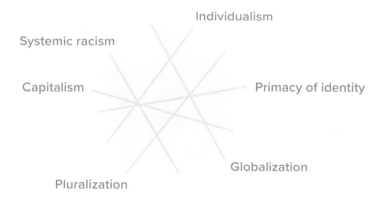

Individualism

Systemic racism

Capitalism

Primacy of identity

Globalization

Pluralization

Globalization expands our obligations to include not just our neighbors but people and communities from around the world. It exposes us to ideas, beliefs, and practices we couldn't otherwise access locally.

Pluralization assumes that we can be at peace as a society and as a world *in light of* our differences, not despite them. People accustomed to pluralization may be able to embrace ideas that seem in conflict on their surface—to live with apparent paradox.

Capitalism creates a consumer mindset with the potential to affect every aspect of our lives, including how we construct our identities. Aspects of one's religious identity, in particular, can be "shopped for," carefully weighed against other options, and then selected—instead of inherited or handed down.

Individualism, the capacity and right to direct one's own self and life, largely makes it possible to have a spirituality unrooted to a particular tradition. It also makes it more difficult, and perhaps more urgent, to determine how and what we owe one another as members of a larger society.

Systemic racism is the subtle, pervasive prejudice at work in individuals and institutions that keeps opportunities and resources aligned with the majority racial or ethnic group and disenfranchises and endangers minority racial or ethnic groups. This kind of racism is embedded in institutions of all types, including religious communities.

Primacy of identity is a term for the way a person's identity or social location, in particular, is itself a form of trustworthy knowledge. Authority or influence in the life of a young person is often filtered by an adult's or an institution's respect for a person's sense of identity.

These forces subtly but substantially impact the fabric of our society. You can begin to see the ways they affect the very stitching of this fabric: how we are bound together, relate to one another, make meaning, build community, make decisions, or construct our identities as a society and as individuals.

WATCH

Watch Dr. Josh Packard discuss inclusion in a Lunch & Learn video with Ellen Koneck.

3

Religious identity, in particular, is impacted by these and other big-picture social and cultural forces. In general, identity today is increasingly seen as something that each individual personally constructs piece by piece, rather than something handed down from a prior generation or imposed by a community. Sophie, 23, a young person interviewed for this report, explains her sense of religious identity:

> I believe in God, but I am not very faith driven. I don't think about religion very often. I don't go to church. Faith is not, unfortunately, a big part of my life. A lot of people get their fulfillment and that meaningfulness through faith, and since that's not a huge part of my life, maybe I'm trying to get it in other ways by helping others. Sometimes I think I would be happier if I were more religious, but I think as long as I'm a good person, helping people when I can, that's really my idea of religion.
>
> Sophie, 23

Sophie doesn't go to church or identify any particular practices that tie her to a specific denomination or tradition. Though a religious institution might contribute to a person's religious identity—in this case, giving Sophie some language for thinking about the existence of God and her personal moral code—young people are increasingly seeking ideas and values from places other than traditional religious institutions.

Of course, this is not true for just Sophie. Her statement illustrates a broad shift among young people: they are moving away from forming religious identity solely through a formal or cultural association with a specific religious tradition. In fact, religious affiliation has declined steadily over many decades. The General Social Survey (GSS) traces this trend starting in 1974, with a steady increase of individuals saying they have "no religion" when asked about affiliation.

The Rise in the Unaffiliated

18–34   35–49   50–64   65+

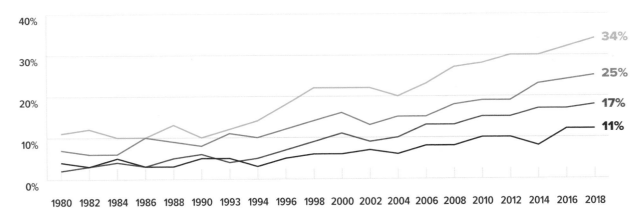

The GSS has been tracing religious unaffiliation in the United States for decades. The data here show those who responded "no religion" when asked about affiliation. It is easy to see the steady rise in the unaffiliated among every demographic, but looking specifically at the gold line — 18-to-34-year-olds — it's obvious that younger generations are disaffiliating (or never affiliating in the first place) at a higher rate.

Springtide data collected in 2020 confirm this larger trend. Nearly 40% of young people ages 13–25 indicate they are unaffiliated, whether agnostic, atheist, or "nothing in particular."

Young people do not necessarily feel that they are bound by the limits of a religion's traditional edges. They take what they perceive to be true, just, and good, and integrate it into a wider worldview.

Cassia, 14, a young woman interviewed by Springtide, describes the ways she is not strictly confined to a particular religious tradition, even while integrating religious practices and beliefs into her life:

> I *do* consider myself religious. I'm a Christian, I do believe that there is a higher power, I'm just not exactly . . . I don't know how to say it. . . . There's a lot of stuff in the Bible that was written there that is kind of weird. I'm not sure how to feel about this. I just believe that everyone should be treated well, forgiven. I'm so bad at explaining my religious feelings. I just want to be a good person, you know, like Jesus' way. I want to be able to help people.

Cassia, 14

Cassia's story begins to get at the complexity—which we will see in even greater detail throughout the report—of the inner and outer lives of young people today.

A CLOSER LOOK

Current Events & Young People

Major social forces impact how young people form their religious identities, as well as how everyone relates to and connects with one another. The work involved in both of these things—constructing identities and building connections—is further complicated by current events. Current events intersect with those social forces, amplifying their impact when it comes to personal and communal beliefs and behaviors.

As with the larger social, religious, and cultural forces at work in the world, a look at what's going on in 2020, specifically, can help make clear the need for a new framework that helps build bonds of trust and lasting impact in the lives of young people today.

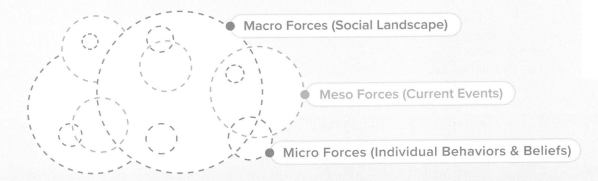

Social forces, current events, and personal beliefs and behaviors intersect and overlap, all impacting young people's religious lives and relationships.

WATCH

Watch Dr. Josh Packard talk with Dr. Eugene C. Roehlkepartain from Search Institute, Sarah Kapostasy from Out Youth, and the team from The Institute for Youth Ministry at Princeton Theological Seminary in the five-part video series *What to Say to Young People During COVID-19.*

4

A CLOSER LOOK

READ

Read in our Voices of Young People blog, our interview with Keziah, 13, about a self-portrait she painted while social distancing.

LISTEN

Listen to Emilie, 26, in *The Voices of Young People Podcast*, talk about the desire for deep conversation.

Coronavirus Pandemic

COVID-19 has changed the way we socialize, learn, work, and lead. It has strained and emboldened our social solidarity and capacity for national discourse. It has forced discussions—of freedom, sacrifice, community, isolation, and what we owe one another—out of the realm of the rhetorical and into everyday life.

When Springtide surveyed young people in March 2020, near the start of the pandemic in the US, **60% said they felt very isolated.**

Increased Connectivity, Decreased Connection

Many in the US and around the world experience increased connectivity but decreased connection. Constant access to news and information, combined with social media and technologies for personal communication, enable ease of communication but not necessarily depth. Though this was true before COVID-19, mandates to shelter in place and social distance exacerbated this experience for many.

Emilie, 26 a young person featured in season 1 of *The Voices of Young People Podcast*, remarks:

 When you have, you know, those connections with peers or whatever and you're texting, . . . you don't get those [deep] conversations as often and you don't get to step outside and grow, and so you just kind of stay rooted to the spot.

Emilie, 26

Record Loneliness

Despite having virtual access to people and places around the world at any time, today's young people are the loneliest on record of any generation.

A study conducted by the global health service company Cigna (2018) that surveyed more than 20,000 US adults ages 18 and older measured the impact of loneliness in America. Among its chief findings was that Generation Z (ages 18–22) is the loneliest generation. Springtide data confirm the experience of isolation and loneliness among young people:

"I Feel Completely Alone"

Percentages of 13-to-25-year-olds by race and age who AGREE (responding "always" or "sometimes")

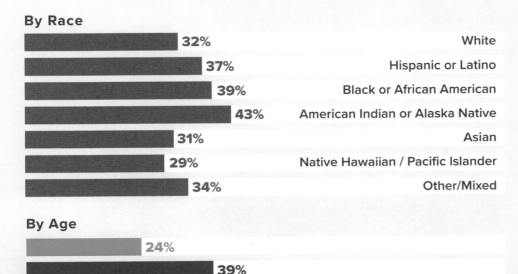

By Race

32%	White
37%	Hispanic or Latino
39%	Black or African American
43%	American Indian or Alaska Native
31%	Asian
29%	Native Hawaiian / Pacific Islander
34%	Other/Mixed

By Age

24%

39%

● 13-to-17-Year-Olds ● 18-to-25-Year-Olds

WATCH

Watch a short video of Dr. Josh Packard unpacking surprising features that play into the epidemic of loneliness.

> Young people today are lonely. Looking at the question of loneliness by race and age, we can learn more about which young people are experiencing isolation.

A CLOSER LOOK

Decline in Religious Affiliation

The steady decline in religious affiliation has been well documented in a variety of longitudinal studies. I*n Belonging: Reconnecting America's Loneliest Generation,* Springtide has also confirmed that participation in religious groups or activities has virtually no protective effect against young people's experience of loneliness.

The GSS graph on page 23, confirmed by Springtide data collected in 2020, makes this trend clear.

Gallup Poll on People's Confidence in Institutions

These numbers represent Gallup's percentages of the US population, 18 years and older, who had "a great deal" or "quite a lot" of confidence in these institutions. Note the severe drop in confidence from the 1970s to 2019.

Institution	1970s	2019
Big Business	26%	23%
The Medical System	80%	36%
The Presidency	52%	38%
Television News	46%	18%
Congress	42%	11%
Newspapers	39%	23%
Public Schools	58%	29%
Banks	60%	30%
Organized Religion	65%	36%

Decline in Trust Across Institutions

Contrary to common conceptions, the decline in trust or affiliation isn't just in organized religion, and it isn't just among young people. Trust in a wide range of institutions is down across every demographic. This includes distrust in government, banks, religious organizations, corporations, and more. To the left is Gallup's poll, comparing trust in institutions across sectors over time. To the right is a breakdown from Springtide focused on young people's trust in institutions, showing little to no trust (on a scale from 1 to 10, with 1 indicating no trust whatsoever) in various institutions.

Young People's Trust in Institutions

Average level of trust of 13-to-25-year-olds in institutions

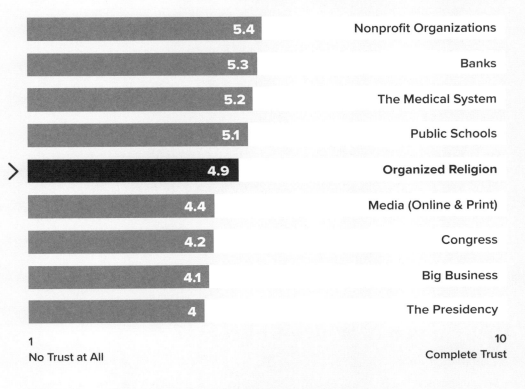

5.4	Nonprofit Organizations
5.3	Banks
5.2	The Medical System
5.1	Public Schools
4.9	**Organized Religion**
4.4	Media (Online & Print)
4.2	Congress
4.1	Big Business
4	The Presidency

1
No Trust at All

10
Complete Trust

> Springtide data confirms what Gallup's poll indicates about trust in various institutions and expands that data set by asking individuals as young as 13 about their experience of trust. With 5.5 as the median between 1 and 10, young people, on the whole, express little to no trust in these institutions.

SPRINGTIDE™ NATIONAL RESEARCH RESULTS
© 2020 Springtide. Cite, share, and join the conversation at *springtideresearch.org*.

Emphasis on Participation & Cocreation

A declining trust in institutions means the work they *used* to do falls to others. If the work of meaning making or community building once fell to religious organizations, it is now the domain of groups like Nuns & Nones, The Dinner Party, boutique and garage gyms, or even the workplace. Related to this, with decreased trust in government, a renewed culture of protests, rallies, and petitions has emerged as civilians take social and political matters into their own hands.

Steven, 22, told us about how he found community in an unexpected place:

> My coworkers and I formed these bonds because we were all hired into the same new place all at once. We just kind of organically formed this community. It was difficult to go away from that job, even when it became something I didn't like because I had to leave behind that community.

Steven, 22

Anti-racism & White Supremacy

Related to the theme of participation and cocreation, 2020 has seen the largest demonstrations in US history. Following the killing of George Floyd in Minneapolis in May of this year, people around the United States and the world protested to support the Black Lives Matter movement and bring sustained national attention to the systemic racism that Black people, Indigenous people, and People of Color have historically endured.

READ

Read about resources for responding to racism in a post featuring suggestions compiled by the members of the Springtide Research Advisory Board.

Abdimalik, 24, lives in Minneapolis. He's an ROTC National Guard member, Somali American Muslim, and is studying political science at a nearby private college. In season 2 of *The Voices of Young People Podcast*, Abdimalik reflects on his experience of being at the epicenter of the conversation around systemic racism:

> I feel like the whole state was affected because recognizing and protesting about racial injustice is something we've been talking about continuously, but it's never really gotten to this level. My friend Mohamed and I were talking about it just the other day, and we came to the conclusion that this has gotten to this point largely because of COVID, in a way, because everyone's now home, you know, without sports or other things to distract you, and you have to see the reality that we're living in. . . . And the fact that there's no distractions means you really have to see the pain and suffering. . . . Personally, my family had to relocate to St. Paul for a little bit, but now, you know, they came back and I'm glad that . . . a conversation is being had.
>
> Abdimalik, 24

Political Polarization

Disagreements about how best to behave in society persist in the United States. Views on the common good—who it's for, what it looks like, how to achieve it—range widely from person to person, creating a climate of political polarization and, often, gridlock.

When asked to describe how they view adults in general when adults talk about politics, young people selected aggressive, dismissive, and disengaged (65%) almost twice as often as they selected considerate and inviting (35%).

LISTEN

Listen to Abdimalik, 24, in *The Voices of Young People Podcast*, talk about his experience as a Black young man in the aftermath of George Floyd's death.

How young people perceive the way adults engage politics

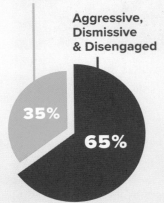

Considerate & Inviting

Aggressive, Dismissive & Disengaged

35%

65%

LGBTQ+ Rights

Conversations, understanding, and policy around gender identity, gender expression, and sexual identity have changed substantially in the twenty-first century. Each has been expanded to include nuance between two traditional, binary categories like man and woman, male and female, gay and straight. These new understandings have informed policies and new civil rights and protections for those who identify as LGBTQ+. Despite these changes, many LGBTQ+ individuals still face difficulties.

Ben, 20, a young person who participated in a qualitative interview with our researchers for this report, remarked on the jarring way his very identity compromises his safety and the kinds of relationships he is able to have:

66 I am transgender and gay, and there are a lot of people out there who would like me to be dead for that.

Ben, 20

Clearly, young people's identities are at stake in the questions, events, and conversations of 2020. A fuller understanding of the factors impacting the ways young people make meaning, construct identity, or form bonds is the foundation for serving them better.

Religiosity: More Complex Than a Checked Box

These factors—large and looming social forces, as well as immediately-felt current events—influence the religious lives of young people. The boundaries around religious practices, beliefs, affiliations, and attendance are blurry for young people. Terms like *religion*, *faith*, and *spirituality* overlap and take on increasingly nuanced meaning.

Springtide survey data show that 61% of young people ages 13–25 report affiliation with a religious tradition or denomination. But a term like *affiliated* doesn't fully communicate the complexity of religious belief and practice for young people today. Even those who tell us they are affiliated with a particular religion may not understand affiliation in the same way a religious leader does. For example, over 50% of those who told us they were affiliated with a religious tradition also report little to no trust in religious institutions (rating trust at 5 or below on a scale of 1–10: no trust to complete trust).

This means that, incredibly, over half of young people who claim an affiliation have little trust in the very religious institutions with which they identify.

The markers that define who is religious and who isn't are not as neat as some might expect. The fact that nearly 1 in 10 of the young people who told us they *were* affiliated with a particular tradition *also* said they were "not religious at all" is indicative of the complexity—the *inadequacy*—of terms like *affiliated* and *unaffiliated* to describe young people's religious identities.

MORE THAN 50% of those who told us they were **affiliated with a religious tradition report** little to no trust in religious institutions.

Over 80%

of young people we surveyed feel that their **life has meaning and purpose** at least sometimes.

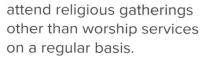

BUT FEWER THAN **1 in 3**

attend religious gatherings other than worship services on a regular basis.

Over 80% of the young people we surveyed feel that their life has meaning and purpose at least sometimes, but fewer than one-third report attending religious gatherings other than worship services on a regular basis. **They are finding meaning and purpose in places outside of religious institutions.**

The complexity of the religious lives of young people becomes even more evident when we look closer at the unaffiliated—the 39% of young people who say they are agnostic, atheist, or nothing in particular. Over 30% of them report that they attend worship services, and nearly the same percentage say they try to live out their religious beliefs in their daily lives. And 60% of the unaffiliated say they are at least slightly spiritual.

In 2020, the broad categories of "affiliated" and "unaffiliated" do not capture the richness and complexity of the inner and outer lives of young people. Religious leaders must meet young people—affiliated, unaffiliated, and everything in between—amid this complexity, even if it means doing so outside their traditional institutions.

The old labels are simply no longer meaningful for understanding the religious lives of young people—if they ever were. According to a Pew Research Center report in 2018, Generation Z is the most diverse generation in the history of America. Service to, and advocacy for, this generation will also be diverse: it will be personal, focused on behaviors rather than prescribed by checked boxes or outdated categories.

When we interviewed Helen, 23, she succinctly explained how her beliefs, behaviors, and identity intersect in a way that illustrates the complexity of navigating a world without many institutional connections:

> I'm not connected to a particular faith, but a generalized faith. I mean, I use prayer, but I don't know that I would connect it to anything certain. I feel like I'm more influenced by trying to do good for humans in general. I don't think it has necessarily anything to do with my spiritual beliefs. I mean, obviously you can see there's a connection, but I feel like it's more about me helping people.
>
> Helen, 23

Like Sophie, mentioned earlier, Helen is pursuing a life of meaning and purpose, but she is doing so without the guidance or structure of an institutional religious organization.

Relational Authority: The State of Religion & Young People 2020 is not a report merely on rates of affiliation and disaffiliation, but an investigation into the religious impulses of young people. Young people you work with. Young people you care about. Young people you are raising or serving or advocating for. Young people like Helen who are trying hard to figure out how to connect the dots in their lives but need trusted guides to help them do it.

We have the data and insights to help you do this work. The following sections of the report include our key findings, a core framework, more in-depth special features, and specific practices to help you respond to the shifting landscape and current complexities that impact young people's religious lives and relationships.

What Young People Are Telling Us

Here's what we know: The inner and outer lives of young people today are complex. Their religious impulses—the things they long for and belong to, the ways they make meaning, construct identity, and connect with others—are more complex than labels like "affiliated" or "unaffiliated" can possibly represent.

WATCH

Watch Dr. Josh Packard discuss the complexities of young people's religious lives and why it's important to focus on behaviors, not just labels.

Because labels fall short, we have to look at behaviors. Social scientists have long demonstrated something called *the intention-action gap*, which is the difference between what we intend to do and what we actually do.

As you can imagine, this gap between intention and action is a reality we have to contend with as sociologists conducting surveys and interviews: People are not always good at predicting their own behaviors. It's not lying, and it's not malicious. It's just hard to predict the future, even when it's our own actions in the future.

This is why Springtide looks at behaviors and beliefs, not just assertions or projections about these things. We ask young people not just whether they claim a religious affiliation, but whether they trust, attend, or practice it in certain measurable ways. We ask young people not just whether they have certain values but how and in what contexts they live out those values.

As we look to understand not just the present, but the implications for the future of religion, religiosity, and religious institutions in America, **it's crucial to consider three intersecting measures of religiosity in the lives of young people—namely: identity, practice, and belief.**

IDENTITY	PRACTICE	BELIEF
71%	**44%**	**55%**
consider themselves to be at least **slightly religious.**	say **attending religious services is important.**	say having **faith in a higher power is important.**

While this report focuses largely on unpacking and complicating the question of identity, there is evidence to suggest that religious practices and religious beliefs are just as complicated.

In the data spreads that follow, you'll see why it's important to unpack and explore these "given" ways of categorizing young people's religious lives. Someone who tells us they are affiliated with a certain religion may also tell us they don't trust religious organizations. A young person may tell us they are unaffiliated while also expressing the ways they live out their religious values in daily life.

These are not contradictions: they are complexities. Grasping these complexities will result in better service to young people—an ability to understand where they are and meet them right there.

DATA

The following pages contain a lot of data. For more breakdowns of data based on race, gender affiliation, and region, go to *springtideresearch.org/thestate2020.*

Here is what's coming in the three data spreads that follow:

KEY FINDING ONE:
Religiosity & Religious Identity

Find rates of affiliation and disaffiliation among young people according to gender and age; note the breakdown of denominations, religions, and traditions with which young people say they affiliate; and observe the distinct ways young people from various traditions talk about their religious and spiritual lives.

KEY FINDING TWO:
Affiliated, Unaffiliated & In-Between

Breaking down the data from Key Finding One, we discover there are young people who say they're affiliated but don't trust religious institutions. Others say they're unaffiliated but attend religious gatherings. So what do affiliated and unaffiliated really tell us? Not much—and certainly not the whole picture.

KEY FINDING THREE:
Meaning, Connection & Relationships

We get a better look at the religious lives of young people by examining their relationships, rather than their affiliation status. How many trusted adults are in their lives? How often do they feel a sense of belonging and community? How do these connections foster a sense of meaning and purpose?

KEY FINDING ONE

Religiosity & Religious Identity

What are young people telling us when it comes to their religious identities? The starting point for a report on the religious lives of young people is straightforward: finding out whether they consider themselves affiliated with a particular religious tradition or not. From this point, we can break down this initial snapshot and see more complex trends emerging that are not represented fully by affiliation status alone.

Religious Affiliation Snapshot

39% Unaffiliated
(Unaffiliated is Nothing in particular, Agnostic, Atheist)

61% Affiliated

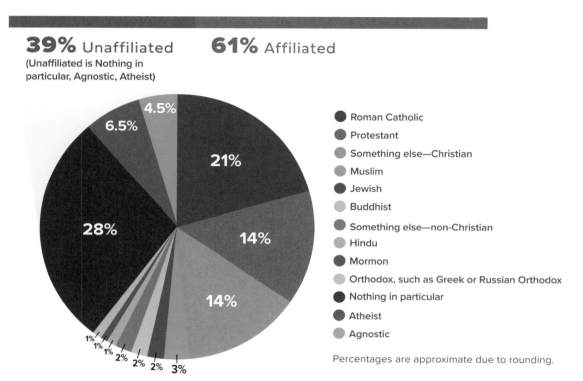

- Roman Catholic
- Protestant
- Something else—Christian
- Muslim
- Jewish
- Buddhist
- Something else—non-Christian
- Hindu
- Mormon
- Orthodox, such as Greek or Russian Orthodox
- Nothing in particular
- Atheist
- Agnostic

Percentages are approximate due to rounding.

Affiliation and Unaffiliation by Age and Gender

AGE

GENDER

13-to-17-Year-Olds   18-to-25-Year-Olds   Male-Identifying   Female-Identifying

● Unaffiliated   ● Affiliated

Religious *and* Spiritual

Percentages of 13-to-25-year-olds who responded "slightly," "moderately," or "very" to questions about being religious and spiritual, according to affiliation

● Young people who say they are religious   ● Young people who say they are **spiritual**

Roman Catholic
- 91%
- 89%

Protestant
- 94%
- 92%

Something else—Christian
- 96%
- 93%

Muslim
- 91%
- 84%

Jewish
- 79%
- 81%

Buddhist
- 81%
- 85%

Something else—non-Christian
- 72%
- 86%

Hindu
- 80%
- 84%

Mormon
- 95%
- 95%

Orthodox, such as Greek or Russian Orthodox
- 82%
- 80%

Nothing in particular
- 47%
- 63%

Atheist
- 11%
- 42%

Agnostic
- 24%
- 65%

Young people who say they are **very religious** and **very spiritual**, regardless of affiliation.

13%
say they are
very religious.

16%
say they are
very spiritual.

"I do not attend any church. I still consider myself someone of faith and someone who has spiritual affiliation, but I do not believe in organized religion."

Chris, 19

"I guess if you have to put a label on it, I'm Christian, but with everything in today's world…I literally don't know. I just think spiritual, maybe?"

Monica, 23

Affiliated, Unaffiliated & In-Between

In the past, it might have been common to assume that if someone claimed "affiliation" with a particular tradition, there was a corresponding set of practices, beliefs, and identities that came along with that designation. That is no longer the case. Nor is the inverse: the unaffiliated are not uninterested in questions of God and meaning; in some cases, they may even be attending religious services or describing themselves as practicing religious values.

SPRINGTIDE™ NATIONAL RESEARCH RESULTS

© 2020 Springtide. Cite, share, and join the conversation at *springtideresearch.org*.

Do you feel that your life has meaning and purpose?

When we asked young people ages 13–25 whether they feel that their life has meaning and purpose, we found that affiliated and unaffiliated young people chose "Never," "Rarely," and "Sometimes" without much significant, statistical difference. But we noted a 13-point spread for those who "often" feel their life has meaning and purpose between those who are affiliated and those who are unaffiliated.

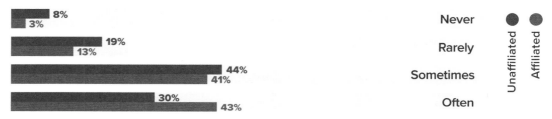

	Unaffiliated	Affiliated
Never	8%	3%
Rarely	19%	13%
Sometimes	44%	41%
Often	30%	43%

Affiliated, but ...

It's easy to assume religious affiliation means trust in organized religion, commitment to a community, attending religious gatherings regularly, or living out religious values. For many affiliated young people, that's not the case.

52% of affiliated young people have **little to no trust in organized religion**.

**20%** of the young people who tell us **they are affiliated with a religious tradition** tell us they **are *not*, however, a religious person**.

Nearly one-third of affiliated young people told us they **do not think it's important to have a faith community**.

33% of affiliated young people **attend religious services once a year or less**.

Over 1 in 5 young people who tell us they are affiliated with a religious tradition also tell us they **don't try to live out their religious beliefs in their daily lives.**

Unaffiliated, but ...

One might assume that a lack of affiliation means a young person isn't interested in questions or lifestyles we often associate with "religion"—including living out religious values or attending religious gatherings. But for a considerable amount of young people, the data tell a surprisingly different story.

 60% of unaffiliated young people say that **they are at least slightly spiritual**.

28% of unaffiliated young people say that they **try to live out their religious beliefs in their daily lives**.

19% of **unaffiliated young people** say that they **attend religious gatherings at least once a month**.

12% of unaffiliated young people say that they have become *more religious over the last 5 years*.

38% of unaffiliated young people say that they *are* religious.

"My Muslim faith does influence my views to an extent because as far as my religion goes, it teaches not to tolerate but to accept. So even though somebody might not agree with me, might not agree with my religion or what it stands for, at the end of the day they're a human being just like I am. And they have their own perspectives and views. Some people might not see it, but a lot of the religions are very similar."

Ayala, 21

What does Springtide mean by *religious*?

For Springtide, the term *religious* is not a reference to a particular creed, code, or system, but rather a term that captures and categorizes a wide array of diverse impulses, questions, and connections. These are the impulses that inspire young people to pursue community, identity, meaning, and connection. And we recognize that these impulses are increasingly finding expression in ways that may not seem overtly religious—that is, they are not connected directly to a specific tradition or institution. Instead, the desire for meaning may show up in careers, club sports, or creative hobbies. Young people find outlets for justice, faith, or purpose in politics, volunteering, nature, and close relationships.

KEY FINDING THREE

Meaning, Connection & Relationships

The places we traditionally look to for forming and guiding religious lives aren't as strong as they used to be. In their place, relationships— including relationships with religious leaders—are all-important. But young people are not always connecting with religious leaders, or in many cases, non-family members at all. Whether affiliated, unaffiliated, or something in between, young people are navigating major questions of identity, meaning, and community. The data show that trusted adults play a crucial role in helping them navigate these questions and concerns.

SPRINGTIDE™ NATIONAL RESEARCH RESULTS

More Revealing than Religious Affiliation? Relationships.

When it comes to mitigating young people's loneliness and helping them feel life is meaningful, relationships tell us more than religious affiliation.

27% of young people have **one or fewer adults in their life that they can turn to if they need to talk.**

31% 18-to-25-year-olds

19% 13-to-17-year-olds

69% have **3 or fewer meaningful interactions in a regular day.**

41% depend on a close relationship **to help them find meaning and purpose in life.**

46% say that their closest relationship(s) **makes them feel like they have meaning and purpose in their life.**

Adults young people could turn to if needed:

Survey participants were able to select multiple answers when asked about this. Consider the small number of religious leaders young people are connecting to, especially compared to other kinds of family and non-family relationships.

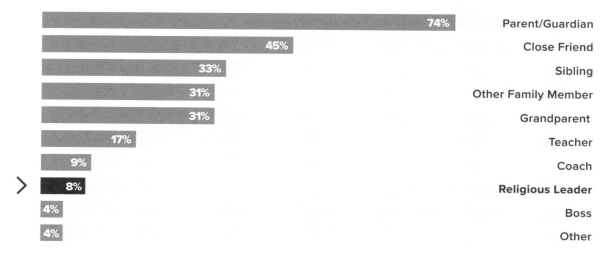

74%	Parent/Guardian
45%	Close Friend
33%	Sibling
31%	Other Family Member
31%	Grandparent
17%	Teacher
9%	Coach
8%	**Religious Leader**
4%	Boss
4%	Other

Mitigating Loneliness & Isolation

Percentages of young people ages 13–25 who respond "always" or "sometimes"

47% are unhappy doing things alone.

48% feel as if no one understands them.

34% feel completely alone.

48% find themselves waiting for people to call, write or text.

38% say no one really knows them well.

39% feel isolated from others.

36% feel shut out and excluded by others.

40% say that people are around them but not with them.

Having adult mentors reduces loneliness

Percentages of young people who responded "sometimes" and "always" that feel they have no one to talk to

● 0 Adult Mentors   ● 1 Adult Mentors   ● 2–4 Adult Mentors   ● 5+ Adult Mentors

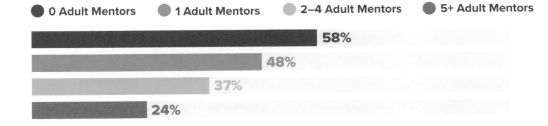

58%
48%
37%
24%

Impact of Relationships

24%

of young people with **no adult mentors never feel like their life has meaning or purpose.**

Just **one adult relationship** reduces that percentage to **6%**.

21%

of young people with **no meaningful interactions per day say that they never feel like their life has meaning and purpose.**

Just **one meaningful interaction** reduces that number to **4%**.

"I've developed beyond religion. Religion isn't as quintessential or as consequential a part of my life as it once was. But that isn't to say that my faith hasn't been involved in why I advocate or don't advocate for a certain individual or issue."

Rich, 23

"I think that there's a greater being. What that greater being is, I'm not really sure, but I think that whatever energy we put out is what we will receive back."

Anastasia, 23

KEY FINDINGS

Summary

The inner and outer lives of young people are complex. In light of shifting social, cultural, and religious forces, and impacted by current events, it's no surprise that the way they form bonds and make meaning is changing. The **Three Key Findings** outlined here make it clear that checking "affiliated" or "unaffiliated" on a survey doesn't tell the whole story of young people's religious identities. It gives us a snapshot—a starting point—but it doesn't tell us all we need to know about the things young people long for and belong to.

When we look closer at behaviors, beliefs, and practices, we discover that affiliated young people aren't always doing the things traditionally associated with religion: attending services, living out particular values, or even trusting the institution they're part of. It's complex for unaffiliated young people too—some of whom do attend religious services or try to live out their religious values. This is why relationships, not affiliation—not membership in a club or even attendance at an organization—can tell us more about the state of religion and young people. Relationships with trusted adults help mitigate loneliness and encourage a sense of meaning and purpose in the lives of young people.

The data show the complexity and nuance of young people's inner and outer lives.

The findings underscore the importance of relationships.

In Part II, we offer a data-driven framework for building relationships with lasting influence that responds to the complexities of the current state of religion and young people. We call this framework Relational Authority.

DATA

There's a lot here. We encourage you to pause and ask questions of the data. If you're reading this online, toggle between the graphs for age, gender, race, affiliation, and region where possible. Think about the young people in your life, and consider how this data informs and enhances what you already know about them. Does it challenge what you thought? Does it align? Are you surprised? energized?

LISTEN

Season 3: *The Voices of Young People Podcast*

Season 3 of *The Voices of Young People Podcast* features ten young people telling us, in their own words, about their religious lives, identities, practices, and beliefs.

Karandeep, 19   Chaltu, 17   Matthew, 24   Hameeda, 23   Jazmin, 25

Mackenna, 19   Kellen, 19   Elijah May, 17   Austin, 16   Kaiya, 19

After the data was collected and analyzed for this report, we spoke with ten young people for *The Voices of Young People Podcast* about some of the themes that arose in our key findings. We asked young people across age, gender, race, affiliation , and region to tell us about their religious lives: What is your experience of the sacred or your image of a higher power? What practices or communities are you committed to, if any? How have relationships impacted your sense of religion or spirituality?

We invited these young people to tell us, with their own voices, about their complex and rich inner and outer lives. The stories they share and the insights they offer are the living, breathing embodiment of these key findings.

The Voices of Young People
PODCAST

PART II

A NEW MODEL
FOR NEW REALITIES
RELATIONAL
AUTHORITY

INTRODUCTION TO PART II

A Framework for Connecting

Part I made clear that young people's inner and outer lives are complicated. By stepping back and looking at the big picture, we start to see how sweeping social, religious, and cultural forces (like pluralism, racism, and individualism) impact how young people develop their identities and bond with others. Looking at the immediately-felt consequences of current events (like COVID-19, rampant loneliness, and a decline in institutional trust), it's easy to see that young people are navigating big questions amid tumultuous times.

It's no surprise that amid these complexities and pressures, the religious lives of young people are more complicated too. Springtide key findings make it clear that affiliation and unaffiliation don't tell the whole story on young people's inner and outer lives. What it means to be affiliated is nuanced. What it means to be unaffiliated is diverse.

**Young people's religious lives are complex, yes.
But they are also rich, exciting, and real.**

Our data also reveal that while navigating all these complexities, young people root their trust in relationship, not institutional authority. **Young people engage and thrive when they encounter trusted adults who care for, listen to, and guide them. Religious leaders are needed to meet young people amid the messiness of the present moment.** To do this work effectively, however, it will be helpful to consider a new approach for connecting with young people. We call this new approach Relational Authority.

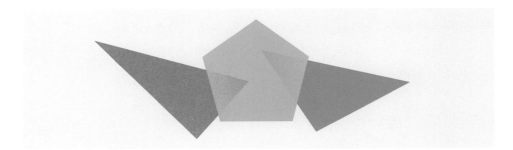

> *The report's cover image symbolizes a way of thinking about different modes of connecting with and influencing others.*

Relational Authority is a framework for connecting with others in light of changing social, cultural, and religious dynamics at work in the world. It is a response to the reality that in a society increasingly connected by impersonal bonds, we often need deep, familiar connection before feeling receptive to the influence or guidance of others. This has clear implications for religious leaders, advocates, ministers, educators, and anyone else caring for the inner and outer lives of young people.

Listening, transparency, integrity, care, and expertise are the five dimensions of Relational Authority.

⬠ Listening is being curious about, engaged in, and remembering what another person said.

⬠ Transparency is sharing experiences, seeking commonalities, and being open with information that impacts others.

⬠ Integrity is following up, following through, being accountable, and being authentic.

⬠ Care is a commitment to the patient and careful work of supporting young people as they navigate questions of identity, community, and meaning.

⬠ Expertise is specialized wisdom and skill that, when combined with listening, transparency, integrity, and care, is the foundation for meaningful relationships.

Intentionally practicing these dimensions is the way to lasting influence in the lives of young people today. This section unpacks Relational Authority as a framework for connecting with young people, offering highly actionable data and practices. These findings and frameworks, combined with our in-depth special features on virtual environments, politics, and careers, can equip and empower you to form connections with young people in ways that respond to real needs arising in light of today's complexities.

Listening

Transparency

Expertise

Integrity

Care

Relational Authority

The *fabric of society,* a term we used in Part I when thinking about the *big picture,* is a helpful image for many reasons. For one, it helps prompt thinking about the way many threads come together to make a whole cloth. At the most fundamental level, shifts in the social, religious, and cultural landscape change the very stitching of this fabric—they change the way we're knitted together as a society. As larger social forces and current events shift, so too do our ways of understanding ourselves and relating to and connecting with others.

Our key findings demonstrate these shifts. We can see nuanced ways of understanding categories of affiliation and unaffiliation in light of shifting behaviors and beliefs, as well as an emphasis on meaning and purpose, often found in or facilitated by trusted relationships.

Part II presents a new model for forging meaningful connections that arises in response to the changing forces in the lives of young people and the impact these forces are having on their religious identities and their relationships. **This new framework is called Relational Authority. Think of it as a new thread that helps stitch us together.**

The need for adult mentors isn't new. Young people want relationships, and they want guidance as they navigate life's big questions. But, in light of larger social factors and current events, the best ways to connect with young people and communicate expertise are shifting. **Young people have a deep need for familiar connection amid a society increasingly glued together with impersonal, transactional exchanges.**

How we are connected, or stitched together, as individuals within society is a question of *solidarity,* which is a term for talking about **a union or bond between people. We are bonded by the sometimes explicit, sometimes implied, commitments we have to one another, which keep our society from fraying at the edges or unraveling altogether**. We may be connected through familial ties or work ties. We might share the same political ideology or the same barber. Our identities reflect these relationships: we are colleagues, friends, siblings, partners, patrons, acquaintances, and more.

DEFINITION

Solidarity is a term for how people are connected to one another, how people are bonded or united. These bonds can be visible or invisible, relational or transactional, rooted in sameness or rooted in difference. No matter how solidarity is forged, its goal is always the same: to keep people bonded.

A CLOSER LOOK

How People Are Connected

The solidarity that holds a society together includes visible connections (connections easily seen or acknowledged) and invisible connections (connections we know exist but don't think much about). For example, when traveling by plane, we are visibly bonded with other passengers as we count on one another to follow flight crew instructions for the sake of everyone's safety. And we're invisibly bonded to those running the air traffic control systems and to the pilots on our plane and on other planes, as we all count on those controllers and pilots to prevent collisions. For a glimpse at the power of social bonds to hold things together, imagine an opposite scene—being on a plane with unruly passengers while approaching an airport to land without the assistance of air traffic controllers. Clearly, these obligations to one anther—visible and invisible—are integral to our thriving on both societal and individual levels.

Similarity & Difference

Sociologists have long offered two ways of thinking about these visible and invisible ties—two ideas about the type of glue that holds society together. One is a solidarity based on what we have in common, and the other is a solidarity based on our differences.

 A **solidarity of sameness** is the social glue that holds a group of (often similar) people together because of what they have in common: beliefs, lifestyle, history, rituals, etc.

Imagine a rural farming community: *Can I borrow your tractor for my fields when you finish using it on yours?*

 A **solidary of difference** is the social glue that holds a group of (often diverse) people together as everyone relies on the distinct skills and expertise of the others.

Imagine an urban US city: *You cut my hair, I'll walk your dog, we'll read this book that she wrote, and he'll watch my kids.*

Both types of solidarity are still at work today: a solidarity rooted in sameness might be the basis for the bonds within a person's immediate family or close relationships, while society at large is stitched together with a solidarity of difference.

Solidarity of Sameness

This type of solidarity is most evident in small societies made up of members with similar lifestyles. While these are more rare in our globalized world, one can imagine largely homogeneous farming communities, for instance, that are stitched together by the rhythms of a common life. Lifestyles—and the rituals and beliefs imbedded within—are held in common. Through this, communities develop deeply ingrained and internalized ways of being together. This bond of collective consciousness is the glue that leads to cooperation. Authority in these communities is *traditional authority* and is typically passed down through generations.

Solidarity of Difference

In a complex society—like much of the modern US—interdependence binds us. A vast network of interrelated services stitches society together. The social repercussions of COVID-19 helpfully illustrate this interdependence and what happens when threads in the fabric are tugged and loosed. For example, when schools closed due to the outbreak, the network that had enabled many working parents to do their jobs and educate and feed their children began to unravel. When considering how much we exchange and depend on others for—not just commodities, but wisdom, skills, ideas—the ways we rely on the labor and presence of others becomes apparent. *Credentialed authority* is what often signals power in this type of solidarity, and, instead of being passed down through families, comes via organizations.

Authority

Authority has a role in each type of solidarity. In solidarity rooted in sameness, one way authority emerges is through **shared experience**: the quality of life among members in this society is so similar that the ability to transmit values and have a positive impact—that is, the ability to have authority—is rooted in a what is held in common. This is typically referred to as traditional authority.

John, 18, explained to our research team how the values he saw modeled by his father became his values—and the basis of a stronger bond because of what they held in common:

 I wanted to be a writer because my dad's a sportswriter. I guess with him, because of his values, he always tries to lead people to be able to tell their story. And have people that share their story for others. And I think that's a good value system, belief system.

John, 18

Mary, 25, felt she could trust someone knowing they had core beliefs in common:

 I knew we had similar beliefs about general worldviews. One of them, I just got to know him better because he was one of the people that I thought I had a lot in common with, and I thought that I could learn from him.

Mary, 25

In solidarity of difference, another type of authority is evident. It comes through **specialized expertise**. Throughout the twentieth century, industries adopted "professionalizing" practices like requiring training, licenses, credentials, or titles as a way to show they had standards for expertise in their field. Today, lawyers, hairstylists, yoga instructors, and religious leaders alike have different certifications to show that they have the authority to do their job. This is often called credentialed authority.

Sal, 18, talks about the importance of expertise when it comes to his relationship with his teaching mentor.

Since I was with her so much in a day, she would throw me into situations where I wanted to have some experience, but also she would talk to me about upcoming career decisions, what to expect, what her experience has been teaching, and how things have changed over time for her, including how what she's learned works for her throughout her years of teaching.

Sal, 18

DEFINITION

We understand **authority as the ability to positively and successfully impact, influence, and transmit values.** Authority, for Springtide, does not mean authoritarian (bossy, dictatorial, or domineering) or authoritative (merely in charge by virtue of having access to power).

A CLOSER LOOK

Just as people in modern society form bonds through both kinds of solidarity, we also rely on and employ both kinds of authority. For religious leaders, commonly held beliefs stitch a community of worshipers together. The leader of a parish, mosque, temple, or synagogue has authority based on being able to speak knowledgeably about something held dearly and in common by all members. That religious leader *also* has authority because they have received training, a specialized degree, a paid position, and a title that sets them apart from a nonspecialist.

But today, we often default to transactional interactions, expecting that our title, degree, or expertise alone can do the heavy lifting when it comes to relationships. The antidote to the transactional is the transformational. The antidote is **Relational Authority**, which is a dynamic exchange of shared experience and sympathetic expertise.

This type of authority emerges as a response to the way society is, outside of family connections, increasingly glued together by impersonal exchanges of goods, skills, or money, instead of *fundamentally* by relationships of care. It demands seeking shared experiences by looking for commonalities even among diverse populations and peoples. It emphasizes the importance of expertise but recognizes that expertise is largely impactful *only after* trust is earned through demonstrated care.

The reality today is that we often default to being transactional in our relationships, assuming trust is a *given* by a title or degree rather than *earned* through relationships of care and wisdom. But we know from our data that . . .

83%

of young people say they are **more likely** to take **advice from someone who cares about them.**

32%

say that **impressive job titles DO NOT matter to them.**

14%

say that if someone has an **impressive job title, they DO NOT trust them.**

We think Relational Authority can change the way leaders relate to, positively impact, and serve the lives of young people. But what is it? 〉

"

I questioned my religion when I was pretty young, but a lot of my questions were kind of shut down by family members too. So, I couldn't really even ask them. But as an adult, probably a few years ago, then I started asking questions again.

"

Lauren, 24

What Is Relational Authority?

Relational Authority is rooted in relationship and earned, not through credentials or titles, but through practices of sympathetic expertise shaped and offered through shared experience. Someone practicing *sympathetic* expertise considers the lived experience of another when deciding the best way to communicate expert wisdom. In this way, someone practicing Relational Authority is humble, aware of their own limitations and listening for signs of shared experience over which to connect, bond, build trust, and share wisdom. They don't assume their expertise or institutional authority has done the heavy lifting when it comes to building connections.

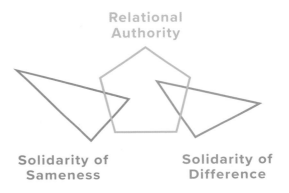

Relational Authority

Solidarity of Sameness   **Solidarity of Difference**

Camille, 23, shared that she trusted her mentors *not only* because they demonstrated a level of expertise in ways she needed as she navigated higher education but also because they showed care:

> I think it was a level of expertise and it was also a shared value system. These were the type of people who I could come to with any problem personally, professionally, academically. I could show up at a meeting 15 minutes late and there would be a high degree of grace and understanding. They put in the work to build a personal connection that made it so that they knew about my life and everything that was going on in it.
>
> Camille, 23

The need for relationships and expertise haven't changed. But, in light of larger social factors and current events, the best ways to connect with young people and communicate expertise is shifting. **Young people have a deep need for familiar connection amid a society increasingly glued together by the division of labor and transactional exchanges.**

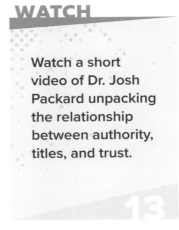

WATCH

Watch a short video of Dr. Josh Packard unpacking the relationship between authority, titles, and trust.

13

Think about it: Beyond family connections, many of the adults in a young person's life—teachers, coaches, youth ministers, counselors—are paid professionals. These adults are connected to young people in a real way not only by the concern that led to a youth-serving profession but also by the paychecks that make it possible. This doesn't diminish the importance of these adults' roles; it does, however, mean that the authority these professionals possess by virtue of title or institutional role is only partial. The authority that makes a difference—that makes it *relational*—has an added element. It is *earned* through care. For religious leaders, advocates, ministers, educators, and anyone else caring for the inner and outer lives of young people, **Relational Authority is a framework based on the understanding that young people often need to feel they are cared for *before they can be receptive to* the influence or authority of others in their lives.**

79%

of young people Springtide surveyed agree with the statement **"I am more likely to listen to adults in my life if I know that they care about me."**

65%

of young people agree with the statement: "A person's expertise doesn't matter if they don't care about me."

Relational Authority is a give and take. Experience and expertise are possessed and shared by both adults and young people in varying degrees at various times. By listening to young people, sharing experiences, looking for commonalities, being forthright, and letting these gestures of openness guide when and how to offer advice or wisdom, trusted adults can have a needed and lasting positive impact on young people today.

Shared Experience, Sympathetic Expertise

If you have ever tried to discuss something controversial on social media, in all likelihood, the conversation didn't get anywhere. The likely reason is simple. Often, a person is receptive to a new idea or opinion only if they feel *you have their good in mind*, that you are not pushing your agenda for your sake—and that if your agenda is wrong, you'll admit it. In short, young people (and all people) want to know that their personhood is the priority, not a point you're making or a program you're pushing. They want shared experience—and the understanding that comes from it—to pave the way for sympathetic expertise to be shared. Because if you can communicate concern for the relationship *first*, receptivity will follow. In fact, trust is a direct result of investing in a relationship in meaningful ways.

87% of young people agree that fostering and working on a relationship is an important part of trust.

What are some of the meaningful ways to invest in and foster deeper relationships of trust with young people? Relational Authority is the framework for cultivating deep relationships with young people that lead to lasting impact and influence. Given that nearly 50% of the young people we surveyed said they feel, at least sometimes, that no one understands them, invested relationships of trust are more urgently needed than ever.

Listening, transparency, integrity, care, and **expertise** are the five dimensions of Relational Authority, and practicing them will help leaders have a positive impact in the lives of young people.

WATCH

Watch a short video of Dr. Josh Packard unpacking how to be a trusted guide—and why that's a big deal.

14

NEARLY **50%** of young people we surveyed said they feel, at least sometimes, that no one understands them.

Practicing Relational Authority

As we've seen through the framework of Relational Authority—a framework that responds to the novel ways young people are forming their religious identities and their relationships—we know young people need to feel that they have a bond, that they are *cared about*, before they are receptive to the guiding influence of people, including and perhaps *especially* religious leaders in their lives. People like you.

How can you form trusted relationships with young people?

How can you build relational authority?

How can you lay a foundation that will lead to lasting impact with a young person?

The five dimensions of Relational Authority are practices rooted in the need to build trusted relationships amid shifting landscapes. These practices are listening, transparency, integrity, care, and expertise.

In the framework of Relational Authority, the emphasis on care does not mean abandoning your expertise. It does not mean abandoning any agenda or advice whatsoever in the name of lukewarm concern. Instead, listening, transparency, integrity, and care should shape when, how, and why expertise is offered.

Those who practice these five dimensions in their relationships can increase their ability to positively and successfully impact, influence, and transmit values to young people. In the last year, Springtide learned that organizations and individuals who embody the dimensions of Relational Authority, as well as other core values we hear from young people, attract young people. **Young people want to feel they belong: They want to feel *Noticed, Named,* and *Known*. Relational Authority is a framework for building this kind of bond through concrete practices.**

In the sections that follow, we demonstrate the importance of these dimensions and the role they play in Relational Authority *and* in the lives of young people. In addition to taking a closer look at these dimensions, we take brief, in-depth looks at the way the framework of Relational Authority aids and intersects with important issues that have emerged in our research, including virtual environments, politics, and careers and vocations. These sections, while brief, are not tangential. As young people's religious longings and belongings shift, expand, and change, religious leaders must be prepared to serve these impulses wherever expressed—including in online gatherings, political discourses, and workplaces.

The *Noticed*, *Named*, and *Known* process comes out of our research on belonging and loneliness. You can read more in *Belonging: Reconnecting America's Loneliest Generation.*

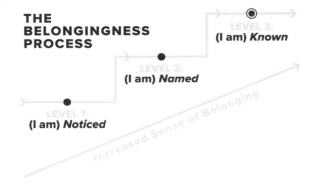

THE BELONGINGNESS PROCESS

LEVEL 3:
(I am) *Known*

LEVEL 2:
(I am) *Named*

LEVEL 1:
(I am) *Noticed*

Increased Sense of Belonging

Listening

Here's a snapshot of what we know from our data about the importance of listening:

"You could sense the connection where I was listening to him and he was listening to me, you know, it was just that listening to one another. I feel like that is what makes a meaningful interaction—when people actually genuinely listen."

Erin, 22

84% of young people ages 13–25 say they will trust someone who remembers things they've shared.

82% say they will trust someone who takes the time to hear what they have to say.

78% of young people say they feel listened to when people show they understand what they've been through.

80% say they feel listened to when people show they care about them.

Young people tell us that listening helps to give rise to trust, which is the foundation for meaningful connections and experiences in their lives. **From over 10,000 survey participants, we learned that 69% of young people have three or fewer meaningful interactions in a regular day.** This is an incredible and devastating statistic. To find out what qualifies, in the experience of young people, as a "meaningful interaction," we asked them. And what we learned is that *listening* is among the most important ways to create a meaningful interaction with a young person.

WATCH

Watch Dr. Josh Packard present a webinar on the importance of relational ministry.

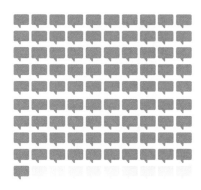

91%
of young people said an interaction is *meaningful* when they feel like they are really being listened to.

Young people view listening as a powerful way to communicate care, build bonds of trust, and have a positive impact in the lives of young people. And it's clear that young people *want* the experience of being listened to. Many (58%) name listening as an *extremely* meaningful type of interaction for them.

"You can go to our teacher for almost anything, and she will keep it very anonymous and quiet—the feeling is very much like, 'I'm here for you, I'll listen to you.'"

Becca, 14

Only about 60% of young people say they almost always have someone to talk to. That leaves about 40% who lack access to someone to talk to when they're making a big decision, celebrating a small accomplishment, stressed, or even lonely. In fact, 7% report they *never* have someone to talk to, and more than a quarter of young people say they have one or fewer adults they can turn to if in trouble and needing to talk.

MORE THAN **25%** of young people say they have one or fewer adults **they can turn to if in trouble and needing to talk.**

LISTEN

Listen to Jana, 21, in *The Voices of Young People Podcast*, talk about trusted adults.

The need for trusted adults in the lives of young people to show up and listen well is urgent. But we are talking about a certain kind of listening, something that goes beyond an efficient exchange of information, or listening in order to respond or retort. We are talking about something deeply attentive and spacious—a type of listening that communicates care.

So what are the hallmarks of this deeper type of listening?

More important, what practices can ensure that it's a *meaningful interaction* in the lives of young people?

Springtide asked young people about different aspects of listening. The qualities that emerged as important are straightforward: being curious, being engaged, and remembering what another person said. Young people consistently said that these qualities gave them the experience of being listened to and heard.

BE CURIOUS through your body language and by asking questions.

81%

of young people say they feel listened to when people seem genuinely curious about what they have to say.

73%

say they feel listened to when people ask questions about what they've said.

 Tide-Turning Tip: Show sincere curiosity through your body language by turning toward the person you're speaking with and nodding along to show that you're following what they're saying. Communication researchers refer to this as having an "open" posture, as opposed to a closed body posture where arms are folded, for example. Ask a few questions before offering a comment or advice. These can be as simple as, "Can you tell me more about that experience, person, or idea?"

BE ENGAGED by focusing your attention on what they're saying rather than preparing your response.

80%

of young people say they **feel listened to when people remain present and engaged as they speak to them.**

75%

say they **feel listened to to when they are allowed the space to say what they need to say without anyone else interjecting.**

 Tide-Turning Tip: Put your phone away (even if the young person you're talking to doesn't). Develop comfort with pauses and silence, which can communicate that you're digesting what they've said, and that you don't have a ready-made response.

Sal, 18, told us about experiences of being listened to in this generous way—and times he's experienced the opposite:

> I've had plenty of good conversations because I could tell that they were listening to understand rather than listening to respond. And there are definitely conversations I've had where I feel like when I'm talking, all they're doing is thinking of how they're going to tell me I'm wrong afterwards.

Sal, 18

REMEMBER WHAT THEY SAID, **and act on it to demonstrate you've heard them.**

78%

of young people told us they feel listened to when people remember what they've said after some time has passed.

82%

say they feel listened to when they see action taken after making a suggestion or complaint.

Tide-Turning Tip: Follow up by asking questions to clarify or repeating what you heard as ways to help your recollection. If your conversation is about actions, jot down notes as a way of showing your intention to follow through.

Felicia, 19, remarks on the felt experience of feeling listened to in all three of these ways. Her sense of belonging is tied to feeling that someone is curious about her, engaged in their conversation, and likely to remember what they talked about.

> "When I think of belonging, I think of being cared for and having someone show any type of genuine interest in how my life is going. When people can remember little things about you or, you know, they remember something that's happened in your life and they'll check in on you around that date— those things definitely make me feel like I fit in with that group."
>
> Felicia, 19

Inquiring, engaging, and remembering are three concrete ways to give young people the experience of being listened to. Combining even *two* of these listening practices increases a young person's feeling of trust toward an adult. This is true across the spectrum of our age demographic.

Listening Builds Trust

Percentages of young people that say they will trust someone who remembers things they shared and takes the time to hear what they have to say

● 13-to-17-Year-Olds   ● 18-to-25-Year-Olds

93%
91%

Giving young people this experience of being listened to is extremely important, as so many feel they don't have someone to talk to, *and* many report so few meaningful interactions in their daily lives. Listening is a meaningful interaction that directly responds to their sense of loneliness and isolation.

Transparency

Young people highly value transparency in their relationships with adults. **It is a practice rooted in sharing experiences in order to discover what is held in common.**

Many religious leaders already know the importance of meaningful connections as young people navigate questions of identity, meaning, and belonging. **Sharing authentically is the only way we can really know and be known by another person.**

People who practice transparency build bonds of trust by sharing experiences and seeking commonalities. Transparent individuals and organizations alike are open about information and ideas that impact others.

DEFINITION

Norms of reciprocity is a term from the social sciences that refers to the way social expectations are established between two people or groups. Essentially, social pressures compel us to "match" someone who has done something for us. At the most micro level, this helps to explain why a person might feel more inclined to open up just after the person they're talking to has shared something personal.

WATCH

Watch a short video of Dr. Josh Packard explaining the need to build trust with young people *and* their families.

SHARE EXPERIENCES by telling stories about your life in ways that encourage others to share.

79% **of young people say they trust someone who shares things about their life.**

 Tide-Turning Tip: "Young people want to know you, not just the institution you represent or the goals and purpose that drive that institution. Sharing personally about the things that matter to you—a friendship that means a lot, the type of music you love, your favorite thing to read, a question you find yourself thinking about—adds human details to any interaction. When shared in ways that maintain appropriate and professional boundaries, these kinds of details can become the basis for trust—which is the foundation for receptivity to new ideas and perspectives.

André, 25, explains the way this kind of sharing from a trusted adult in his life helped him open up:

 There was a lot of genuine sharing with my mentor. Naturally, I'm not a person to speak first, so when they were vulnerable with me, I felt safe to be vulnerable with them. Sharing hard situations, hard stories in their lives. That vulnerability created that space for me.

André, 25

SEEK COMMONALITIES in order to develop mutual understanding.

80%

trust those who understand their lived experiences.

DEFINITION

In-groups is a term from the social sciences that refers to the group of people with which a person identifies closely. *Out-groups* are everyone else. One of the defining features of in-groups is that members of in-groups are much more open to influence and suggestions by fellow in-group members and maintain a distinct resistance to influence from out-group members.

Tide-Turning Tip: Seeking commonalities follows sharing experiences for a reason. It's only when you start sharing that you can discover the nuanced ideas, hobbies, friends, or favorite foods to bond over. Because experience is a form of knowledge, having someone who has gone through similar things in life gives authority to speak into and from those places of shared understanding.

Glenn, 23, seeks out commonalities as a basis before receiving the guidance of another:

 I have always found a way to have a prior relationship or common footing with those I'm seeking advice from.

Glenn, 23

INCLUDE OTHERS **by being open with information.**

87%

say they trust someone who tells them what is going on and makes sure they feel included.

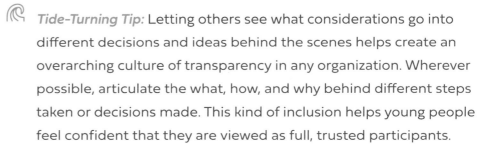 *Tide-Turning Tip:* Letting others see what considerations go into different decisions and ideas behind the scenes helps create an overarching culture of transparency in any organization. Wherever possible, articulate the what, how, and why behind different steps taken or decisions made. This kind of inclusion helps young people feel confident that they are viewed as full, trusted participants.

Practicing the dimension of transparency in more than one of these ways increases the sense of trust a young person feels toward that adult.

Transparency Builds Trust

Percentages of young people that trust someone who models transparency by sharing personally, understanding life experiences, and keeping them informed of things.

● 13-to-17-Year-Olds　　● 18-to-25-Year-Olds

92%

86%

Ashley, 23, talked to Springtide about a trusted adult in her life who modeled these elements of transparency—how this mentor was a guide through her openness in both professional and personal ways:

> I definitely had a really good mentor in college. She was my boss for the campus job that I was doing and she was just a great mentor. Initially, I was drawn to her professionalism. She really knew what she was doing—she can lead meetings and that was really appealing to me. But beyond that, she's just extremely open and hospitable to individuals. Going through college, I went through a lot of stuff with my family, and she was a good mentor in my personal life too, providing comfort and stability.
>
> Ashley, 23

Given the default, superficial, and often transactional ways we're connected as a society—coupled with the complexity of any one person's religious longings and belongings—the work of transparency is crucial for deep and meaningful bonds. Practicing this dimension of Relational Authority is a critical way for trusted adults to begin forming these kinds of bonds.

Integrity

Adults with integrity follow up and follow through in their relationships with young people.

Integrity is a core dimension of Relational Authority because following up, following through, being accountable, and being authentic are ways to demonstrate a stable and committed presence in the lives of young people. Amid superficial or fleeting connections throughout society, bonds rooted in integrity are foundational for lasting influence.

FOLLOW UP with young people in ways that show you care about their needs.

85%

of young people say that their trust in another person grows when that person takes action that responds to the young person's needs.

 Tide-Turning Tip: Following up with young people starts with remembering what was exchanged—a hallmark of listening and a foundational aspect of Relational Authority. Track events and milestones for each young person on a spreadsheet or list and set reminders. If they have a big test coming up, wish them luck just beforehand. If they are making a difficult decision, check in and offer to be a sounding board.

For Ophelia, 20, a relationship based on checking in and following up on life in general, including bigger questions of meaning, are the basis for a strong relationship in her life:

> My check-ins with him every week to hear about his life and talk about philosophy or just the meaning of life and random ideas turned into a really cool friendship.
>
> Ophelia, 20

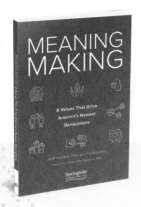

In *Meaning Making: 8 Values That Drive America's Newest Generations*, Springtide explains and explores the values young people told us matter most to them, including accountability, authenticity, and others. The book is packed with data, definitions, narratives, and tips for taking action. In addition to the book itself, we've produced resources to help you or your organization reflect on and implement these values into your culture. A podcast series, webinars, blog posts, a Lunch & Learn video series, and more are all available for free on our website.

FOLLOW THROUGH with commitments.

82% of young people trust someone who does what they say they are going to do.

Tide-Turning Tip: Follow-through is at the heart of integrity, and integrity is at the heart of trust. It is a simple but important practice of doing what you say you're going to do. Don't overstate commitments that will be hard to keep, and keep all the commitments you make. If you commit to something big, break it down into steps and note deadlines for yourself.

BE ACCOUNTABLE by taking responsibility for mistakes.

83% trust someone who takes action to fix things when they've caused harm.

Tide-Turning Tip: Everyone makes mistakes, and young people don't have an expectation of perfection from the adults in their lives. But they do expect accountability. The best ways to ensure accountability are through clear expectations, shared purpose, and forums for feedback.

18

BE AUTHENTIC by admitting what you don't know.

80% of young people trust someone who admits when they are wrong.

 Tide-Turning Tip: Admitting that you're wrong is a humbling process, but authenticity is characterized by the ability to be yourself without worry about performing a certain way—including always being right. Practice getting comfortable with "I don't know." The limits of your knowledge are opportunities to learn more from the wisdom of others.

People with integrity practice what they preach; they walk the talk. They take accountability for their actions and strive to live lives free of hypocrisy. By doing these things, a trusted adult can be a stable presence in this often tumultuous, always complex season of growth for young people. When an adult does all these things—actively practices following up, following through, being accountable, and being authentic—young people overwhelmingly indicate a strong sense of trust for that adult.

Integrity Builds Trust

Percentages of young people who tell us they trust people who model and practice integrity through following up, following through, being accountable, and being authentic

● 13-to-17-Year-Olds   ● 18-to-25-Year-Olds

94%
91%

DEFINITION

The desire to maintain the power—and status that comes with being "right"—is so strong that social scientists have coined the phrase **techniques of neutralization** to explain the lengths we go through to avoid owning mistakes, including mistakes we might, in similar circumstances, otherwise hold others accountable for.

"You have got to have the ability to say I did this wrong. I learned from it for the future. I won't make a similar mistake."

Luke, 23

Care

Young people want to know you care. They want to know you are invested in the relationship in a serious, committed way.

87%

of young people say they trust adults who take time to foster relationships.

81%

of young people say they will trust someone whom they believe cares about them.

WATCH

Watch a short video of Dr. Josh Packard discussing care.

But what is care?

Care can be demonstrated in some of the ways we've discussed in previous sections on listening, transparency, and integrity. Things like following through on ideas or conversations, seeking commonalities, or showing genuine curiosity can all be acts of care. But unlike the other dimensions of Relational Authority, care is bigger than discrete actions.

To care for young people is to want and work for their flourishing. It's a commitment to the patient and careful work of supporting them as they navigate questions of identity, community, and meaning. It is a willingness to meet them amid the messy and complicated array of social forces, current events, and religious impulses they experience and to seek to guide and accompany them.

It's hard to imagine being a trusted adult in the life of a young person and not possessing the quality of care. The two are almost synonymous: a trusted adult *is* a caring adult; a caring adult *is* trusted. To dig deeper, imagine what sets caring teachers apart from other teachers. The role of a teacher is fundamentally rooted in helping young people, and both kinds of teachers are trusted adults. A caring teacher, though, will not just communicate ideas and lessons to students but will also show concern for their well-being outside the classroom.

Camille, 23, told Springtide about the role of caring adults during her education. Her teachers went above and beyond the responsibility to *teach*, showing care for Camille as a person—someone juggling new commitments, information, responsibilities, health concerns, and career decisions. One teacher, in particular, insisted on her flourishing—even through unconventional means.

See her story on the next page. >

"I had a few very difficult experiences during my undergraduate years because of my health, which meant my relationships to teachers weren't really always a matter of advancing a career. They were a matter of making sure I was healthy and safe and all of those things. I think that's why radical empathy was so huge for me. I was coming into contact with new identities. They were navigating this space with me as a part of their support for me.

One time I was doing an independent study with my favorite professor, and he said: "Your homework this weekend is to watch three episodes of the Kardashians and tell me about them." And I was like, "I hate the Kardashians." And he was like, "I know, but I need you to take a break somehow and prioritize yourself."

Camille, 23

So how can adults *show care* to the young people in their lives?

Because care is an underlying commitment, you can express it in almost unlimited ways in your relationships with young people:

- Talk with them and really listen.

- Remember their birthday, a particular milestone in their life, or perhaps their favorite movie.

- Advocate for them or give advice.

- Speak up for them or give them a platform to use their own voice.

Whatever you do, your care for young people will not only make your actions meaningful but also help young people feel more receptive to you.

In fact . . .

83% of young people say they are more likely to take advice from someone they know cares about them.

79% say they are more likely to listen to adults in their life if they know those adults care for them.

When asked what made her trust her mentors, Amelia, 21, said:

> I think they really cared. I could feel that they really cared about me and my emotional and mental well-being and not just like making sure I succeeded academically. They were always willing to listen and weren't trying to push their own agenda on me. I trusted them just because of the great feedback they gave me on different things, and they were available to meet with me and prioritize that time.
>
> Amelia, 21

"If you come in as a teacher and they only know you as a robot who just teaches about history, then they're not going to care. But if you 'get' them—if you work hard to understand them—they're going to care and they're going to listen to what you're saying."

André, 25

André, 25, has been a mentor and a mentee. His experience confirms that showing care *first* makes others receptive to whatever new information or idea you are presenting.

As Camille, Amelia, and André express, practicing care is not vague or sentimental. It's not a hollow expression of concern—and it's *not* a given just because someone works with young people. Instead, it is a concrete commitment to the flourishing of the young people in your life. This commitment lays important groundwork for a young person to trust and be receptive to the guidance and influence of a trusted adult in their life.

When it comes to religious impulses and desires for meaning, community, and identity, every individual will flourish in different ways. Likewise, care will look different in every relationship.

Expertise

Listening

The final dimension of Relational Authority is expertise. We present it last because young people need to feel they are cared before they are receptive to the expertise, advice, or wisdom of the adults in their lives. In this sense, expertise follows after care, integrity, transparency, and listening have laid the groundwork in a relationship. >

LISTEN

Listen to Jana, 21, in *The Voices of Young People Podcast*, talk about meaningful relationships.

20

65%

**of young people agree with the statement,
"A person's expertise doesn't matter**
if they don't care about me."

This doesn't mean young people don't want guidance and advice.
It doesn't mean expertise doesn't matter. Young people just want
it from someone they already trust *wants their flourishing.*

It isn't surprising that so many young people agree that a person's expertise doesn't matter if that person doesn't care, first—especially given the many ways our society is stitched together with transactional ties. When expertise *follows* care, it can be shaped by care. When advice *follows* listening, it can be personalized. When guidance *follows* integrity, young people can trust that the guide is trustworthy.

We sometimes call this *sympathetic* expertise, because it considers the lived experience of another before deciding the best way to communicate expert wisdom. Someone practicing Relational Authority is humble, aware of their own limitations and listening for signs of shared experience over which to connect, bond, build trust, and then share wisdom.

Adults practicing Relational Authority don't assume their expertise has done the heavy lifting when it comes to building connections, because expected forms of expertise often *aren't* compelling on their own: Only about a quarter of young people say that attributes such as being clearly in charge (27%) or having an impressive job title (26%) are significant factors in making them trust a person. Even fewer (21%) see having a large social media following or a lot of money as reasons for trust.

Some traditional markers of expertise are still important to young people. For example, 70% of young people say they are likely to trust someone who has had a lot of training or education in their field. Much *more* important than relying on any "given" authority is the way authority is used. That's where listening, transparency, integrity, and care come in.

> This is the heart of expertise shaped by care. When a person listens first, they can respond to needs they might not have fully understood if they led with advice or expert explanation.

Care Shapes Expertise

84%
of young people say they trust someone who not only knows a lot but also uses that knowledge to help them.

What does this look like?

Faith formation programs are often regimented by a prescribed time line—certain lessons are presented in the elementary years, others during the middle school years, and eventually young people "graduate" from religious formation with some ritual of adulthood. But these prescribed time lines may not match what's going on in the life of a young person. Given what we know about the complexity of young people's religious lives, not to mention factors impacting socioeconomic situations, access to resources, or sense of external stability, religious formation program designers have to consider that it's often more than likely that these time lines *don't* match where a young person is in their development. Imagine, instead, a formation program guided by experts that permits and encourages spiritual progress at a pace dictated by the young person. Even on a small scale, imagine creating single rituals to mark seasons of the young person's life. Responsive to the needs, desires, hopes, and impulses they experience, these kinds of thoughtful markers can meet young people precisely where they are at in life.

Shared Experience Shapes Trust

80%
of young people say they are more likely to trust someone who knows what it's like to experience what they've been through in their own lives.

What does this look like?

Imagine a liberal arts professor trying to break through to a student who is in college to get a good job, but who feels time and tuition are wasted on the liberal arts. Jordan, a student at a public university in the western United States, found no value in engaging with a required liberal arts class—it simply didn't help in practical ways to get ahead on a career path—and Jordan did not trust the professor. Imagine the professor listening and hearing the student's anxieties, seeking ways to relate to the experience by reflecting on their own. Practicing integrity and transparency, this professor figures out a way to appeal to Jordan's practical concerns and constraints. And the professor's show of care by using expertise in a way that appeals to and reassures this student makes it more likely that Jordan can thrive in the classroom.

This doesn't mean a person has necessarily gone through all the same life experiences as a young person. Rather, it means taking the time to learn about the life experiences of another—of young people, in their own words—to better cater any influence, advice, or ideas to the exact moment they're at in their lives.

Relational Authority is earned through listening, transparency, integrity, and care. It is expressed through expertise. When all five of these dimensions are practiced by adults, young people are receptive and willing to trust them.

Young People Trust Adults who Practice All Five Dimensions of Relational Authority

A closer look at how young people of various ages indicate trust based on the five dimensions of Relational Authority

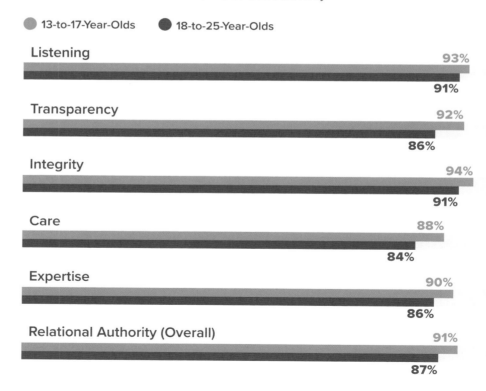

● 13-to-17-Year-Olds   ● 18-to-25-Year-Olds

Listening
93%
91%

Transparency
92%
86%

Integrity
94%
91%

Care
88%
84%

Expertise
90%
86%

Relational Authority (Overall)
91%
87%

Impact of Relational Authority by Race

A closer look at how young people of various races indicate trust based overall the five dimensions of Relational Authority

White — 89%

Hispanic or Latino — 90%

Black or African American — 86%

American Indian or Alaska Native — 78%

Asian — 93%

Native Hawaiian / Pacific Islander — 92%

Other — 91%

Our data show that regardless of race, young people trust adults who practice the dimensions of Relational Authority.

For religious leaders, advocates, ministers, educators, and anyone else caring for the inner and out lives of young people, it is crucial to realize that young people often need to feel cared for before they can be receptive to the influence or authority of others in their lives. This doesn't mean expertise isn't needed—quite the opposite. While young people navigate major questions in life, they want and need trusted adults to guide them.

A CLOSER LOOK

VIRTUAL ENVIRONMENTS & YOUNG PEOPLE

Gatherings that traditionally take place in person are, and have been, moving online. COVID-19 has accelerated this phenomenon. Meeting for school, work, or worship through a virtual environment is widespread, and it will be a reality for the foreseeable future.

To successfully navigate the shift from in-person to online gatherings, leaders must maintain a sense of community, belonging, and meaningful connection among those gathered.

How do we make sure virtual environments are *transformative* and not just *transactional*?

Our data, collected in June 2020, indicates the importance of this task across all institutions, including churches, mosques, synagogues, and other religious organizations as well as schools and workplaces.

WATCH

Watch a short video of Dr. Josh Packard explaining the difference between isolation and choosing to be alone.

21% of young people have been in virtual environments for religious gatherings.

32% have gathered remotely with friends.

21% of young people have met online for work.

64% have participated in a virtual environment for school.

Others added that they have participated in workout classes, therapy sessions, doctor appointments, committee meetings, and even weddings online.

Despite the now-common experience of these activities happening virtually, young people are experiencing a disconnect online:

61% of young people said that they felt disconnected from people in a virtual setting.

47% of young people said that they didn't feel heard or listened to in a virtual environment.

57% of young people said that they didn't feel like they could ask questions of authority figures in these spaces.

A CLOSER LOOK

This sense of disconnection is more pronounced for 13-to-17-year-olds: Sixty-five percent say they feel disconnected in virtual settings, while 59% of 18-to-25-year-olds feel the same way. The sense of not feeling heard is less pronounced for 13-to-17-year-olds: 41% say they don't feel heard, while 50% of the older group (18–25) in our demographic tell us they don't feel heard.

Holly, 20, told us about difficulties of suddenly switching to virtual learning and working when coronavirus first required sheltering-in-place:

 Right now I'm interning with a public accounting firm and I would have spent the summer in the city, but they just moved it all remote. So I'm just doing it from my home. I *would* have been at an audit—I would have been interacting with clients and there would have been social interactions. But just being in the basement of my house is like a full 180. Now you just like talk to people over like Zoom or Teams. It's all like screen stuff. So that's been like a difficult adjustment. But I've been getting through the best I can.

Holly, 20

In the shift to virtual environments, young people have felt a loss. They don't feel connected, listened to, or sure how to recreate certain relational dynamics, like asking questions. This loss is felt keenly among those hoping to connect with their faith communities online. Leah, 20, says:

 I've been watching sermons online, which is good, but obviously not the same as if I were going to church.

Leah, 20

It is—and it will be—hard work to build community, *especially* religious community, in new and nuanced online spaces. But the work won't be in vain. Young people are willing to invest in these spaces for the long term.

67%

said they would learn to adjust to the virtual setting if they had to.

47%

said they would be fine if their school experience remained in a virtual environment.

Not only are they willing to invest in and commit to creating meaningful virtual environments, they see some opportunities among the losses. Brianna, 23, told Springtide about her experience of connecting with her faith in an online setting:

I find meaning through my church community, and it's definitely a different sense of community given the times we're in and how we're finding meaning. There's something to be said about physically being with people, but COVID-19 has also opened up opportunities to connect with people virtually or on the phone that I haven't connected with in a while. So, building and strengthening a community that exists, I see as an opportunity.

Brianna, 23

A CLOSER LOOK

Faith leaders should also see an opportunity. In our Social Distance Study, a small study conducted in the first weeks of sheltering in place and social distancing, Springtide asked young people how the pandemic and the surrounding social conditions were impacting their faith.

How is the pandemic impacting your faith?

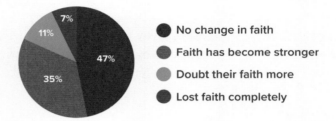

- ● No change in faith
- ● Faith has become stronger
- ● Doubt their faith more
- ● Lost faith completely

7%
11%
47%
35%

All these data points can prompt religious leaders.

- How can you encourage and serve the growth already at work in the 35% of young people who say their faith is getting stronger?

- How can you sustain and deepen the faith of those young people whose faith is steady amid these external changes?

- How you can reach out to and anchor those who are experiencing doubt in their faith lives?

- And finally, how can you do all of this *virtually*?

The principles of Relational Authority—listening, integrity, transparency, care, and expertise—remain important for positively impacting young people in virtual settings. How these dimensions find expression online requires some creativity. ❯

LISTEN

Listen to "Panorama for Orchestra," created by Conner, 23. He composed this piece in response to the question "How are you finding connection and meaning in these days of physical distancing?" Read our interview with him in our Voices of Young People blog.

VIRTUAL ENVIRONMENTS & YOUNG PEOPLE

Tide-Turning Tips:

1. Host virtual gatherings that engage groups of different sizes, for different purposes, including small groups, large groups, and one-on-one conversations, if appropriate. It can be hard to know how and when to speak up on a Zoom call with a dozen or more other people, but different dynamics are possible through gatherings of different sizes.

2. In addition to the digital, think about the analog. Write letters or postcards, even encouraging the young people in your care to write letters to one another.

3. Try to make gatherings more personable. Consider having pet-, partner-, or family-friendly practices, talent shows, or even icebreakers that foster relationship building.

4. Think about the casual kinds of conversations that happen before or after a formal gathering, and be intentional about making space for "unscheduled" connecting. Use your screen to pose a question that individuals can think about as they log in, share with the group, or respond to in a chat message to get casual conversations going before or after the main reason for gathering.

5. Highlight how you're learning and growing amid new circumstances, including the ways your expertise and education perhaps didn't prepare you for the tasks at hand, whether that relates to learning new technologies or working from a new environment. Let young people be cocreators of the space you're building, and ask for help with resources and ideas for better ways to connect and bond.

While the young people we surveyed feel the loss of in-person gatherings, they recognize that this shift toward virtual environments may be here for the foreseeable future. Because of that, they are willing to invest in these spaces. You can too. Transformational, rich, and long-lasting relationships are not only possible but crucial in virtual environments.

A CLOSER LOOK

A CLOSER LOOK

POLITICS & YOUNG PEOPLE

Older people, like our parents, don't really listen. They half listen to our opinions, thoughts, whatever the case may be. They don't really hear us out.

Alyssa, 19

Politics is the realm where our private concerns, values, and beliefs are made public. It is important for religious leaders, parents, and other trusted adults to engage young people about the ways they express their inner and outer lives in political discussion and activities.

When we broke this finding out by age,

47%

of 13-to-17-year-olds— who cannot yet legally vote—tell us they know more than adults give them credit for.

52%

of young people say they know more about politics than adults give them credit for.

45%

of young people say they wish the adults in their lives would let them into the conversation about politics more often.

Religious leaders, in particular, have an opportunity. **While 65% of young people indicate that their faith affects their involvement in politics at least a little, many say that faith leaders (46%) and houses of worship (42%) in their lives have had *no impact* on their involvement in politics. While faith may be informing their politics, for many young people, faith *leaders* are perceived as uninvolved.**

Additionally, adults throughout their lives are often modeling how to talk about politics in unhealthy ways. When asked how they find adults in general when they talk about politics, young people selected **aggressive, dismissive, and disengaged (65%)** almost twice as often as they selected **considerate and inviting (35%)**. Forty-one percent of young people feel that most adults in their lives disregard their feelings about political issues.

These twin factors of poor modeling and dismissiveness only serve to heighten divisiveness in an already polarized political climate. Adults are missing opportunities to deepen values, religious beliefs, and ethical commitments when they don't engage young people in political conversation in healthy, respectful ways—or engage them at all.

Adults who *do* encourage and invite political conversations—largely parents and other family members—are seizing an opportunity to have meaningful, robust, and relational exchanges with the young people in their lives. We found that the the differences between the average adult in a young person's life (who is perceived to be dismissive or disengaged) and the trusted adults, (who are considerate and inviting) are rooted in the practices of Relational Authority.

How young people perceive the way adults engage politics

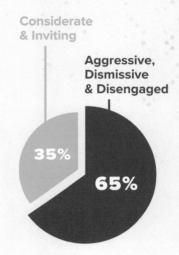

Considerate & Inviting

Aggressive, Dismissive & Disengaged

35%

65%

"I have had very few healthy political conversations in my lifetime. Nobody wants to listen. They just want to talk."

Corey, 21

Politics & Relational Authority

Our data suggest that practicing the values of Relational Authority—listening, transparency, integrity, care, and expertise—can help trusted adults do a better job effectively engaging, encouraging, and understanding the political impulses of young people.

PRACTICE LISTENING: As mentioned on the previous page, 41% of young people ages 13–25 feel like most adults in their lives disregard their feelings about political issues, and many find adults to be dismissive, disengaged, and aggressive. Listening starts with acknowledging that young people have political ideas and opinions, and inviting them into conversation about those concerns.

PRACTICE TRANSPARENCY: Fifty-nine percent of the young people Springtide surveyed say that personal experiences make them passionate about political issues. Learning about those personal experiences—and sharing your own—is a way into political conversations with young people. Rather than using scripted talking points around issues, try starting conversations around why an issue matters to you.

PRACTICE INTEGRITY: Sixty-eight percent of the young people Springtide surveyed say that they would not stop speaking to someone who strongly disagreed or opposed their political values, and 77% want to be having conversations about differences openly. Although young people aren't intimidated by disagreement, they need adults to model open-minded dialogue that doesn't shun, shame, or disown others for having diverse perspectives. Commit to a having a discussion with real integrity by entertaining and learning more about ideas and opinions you may not hold.

"I try not to get into politics with certain people because they aren't open minded, you know, having a debate, seeing the perspective of another, even acknowledging they still disagree after listening."

Ayala, 21

PRACTICE CARE: Seventy-seven percent of young people say that they are most comfortable engaging with friends, parents, and trusted adults about how to find different points of view on political and social issues on the internet. A foundation of trust makes sharing experiences and discussing difficult topics safer and easier to do. If you are a trusted adult in the lives of young people and they feel they can come to you with a range of other concerns, try inviting them into political conversations.

PRACTICE EXPERTISE: Eighty-one percent of young people say it is important to try to understand both sides of a political issue, and 84% of young people agree that getting educated about the views and perspectives of others is important for seeing both sides more clearly. Modeling a humble expertise means listening, considering the experience of others seriously, and committing to continued education and dialogue.

Political conversations are a chance to explore and express deep values that emerge out of experience and expertise. **Young people aren't afraid of contentious issues or difficult topics**—but they are missing models of productive, healthy dialogue from many adults in their lives. Religious leaders can show up to this space by practicing Relational Authority.

"I feel like most of the adults that I've talked to about politics are people that I'm related to. I definitely feel respected by all of them. I feel like I am listened to."

Steve, 21

"I know that I want to be in a profession where I feel like I'm making a difference and I'm in contact with people and actually doing things with my hands to serve other people and listen to their stories."

Leah, 20

CAREERS & YOUNG PEOPLE

Young people are seeking to live meaningful lives. But where and how they find, express, and make meaning is changing.

Work is one of the places that young people are expressing and enacting their values. It's a place where many are pursuing a sense of purpose. It's a place they can build community and find belonging.

91%

of young people ages 13–17 want their future work to be meaningful, and they want a job that helps them grow as a person.

87%

of young people ages 18–25 say that contributing to something important and meaningful at their workplace would give them a sense of belonging.

Findings from our study on careers and vocations suggest that work is a place of meaning and belonging, and young people want guidance and mentorship when it comes to career decisions. Sixty-two percent of young people ages 18–25 wish they had someone to talk to about their professional future. Younger individuals, ages 13–17, feel that they can talk to their parents (80%) or to their friends (67%) about jobs they'll look for in the future, but they don't turn to religious leaders to discuss these things. In fact, religious leaders were ranked the second lowest, at only 8%, of any type of relationship when we asked 13-to-17-year-olds who they talk to about their future work lives.

Faith in the Workplace

● 13-to-17-Year-Olds   ● 18-to-25-Year-Olds

 72%

 56%

 73%

Of those who indicate they follow a faith, 72% say their faith plays at least a small role in how they plan for their future job.

56% of young people say that faith plays at least a small role in how they make plans for future work.

73% of young people say it is at least somewhat important to them to live out their faith at work.

Because religious leaders are often already equipped for discussions of thoughtful decision-making, personal gifts and skills, and meaningful work, they are perhaps better positioned than many other trusted adults to play a role in these conversations. This means that even though our data suggest young people aren't currently turning to them, religious leaders have an opportunity. They have a chance to engage young people in discernment about careers and vocations, especially because young people seek to incorporate their sense of religious values into their daily work.

WATCH

Watch a Lunch & Learn video with Dr. Josh Packard and Ellen Koneck discussing what attracts young people to organizations.

23

A CLOSER LOOK

Viewed as a space of meaning and community, it's understandable that young people want to talk about work. And it's perhaps also unsurprising that nearly 70% of 18-to-25-year-olds feel *called* to a specific career.

Ashley, 23, explains the way naming her own strengths helps her feel a sense of calling:

 From a broader point of view, I believe that we are all given gifts and that we are asked to use those gifts to better the world and make it a place that is kind and loving. I think that's easy too, to recognize what your gifts are and then apply them. I think that makes it easier for me to know what my job is supposed to be and know what my calling is.

Ashley, 23

Adam, 23, echoes this sense of calling at work:

 I think that's a big question: where am I being called to go? I think this calling can really impact just about every other part of your life. And you can choose to be unhappy because of the work that you do, or you can realize what your passions are and where there are needs you can do something about. You're going to find fulfillment and joy in following your passions and that will bring to joy to other parts of your life.

Adam, 23

But for some reason—with the exception of attending to a sense of calling *to a religious job*—it often seems as though religious leaders have exempted themselves from engaging young people in conversations and guidance about careers. At least, this seems to be a perception among young people, who are turning to school counselors, parents, and peers about career conversations at much higher rates than they turn to religious or faith leaders.

While it may be common to talk about careers or vocation when it comes to a young person discerning a specific religious career or path, faith leaders have an opportunity to engage young people more broadly about work as a place they are finding and making meaning, purpose, belonging, and connection. As young people express their religious impulses outside the confines of specific religious institutions or traditions, religious leaders can show up to those new spaces as guides.

Whether helping a young person weigh a difficult career decision, find a job that allows them to live out their values *and* use their degree or training, or discern their own natural gifts, religious leaders have much to offer young people in conversations about work.

A CLOSER LOOK

Conclusion

Springtide understands religion broadly. And we know that the religious lives of young people are more complicated than the labels "affiliated" or "unaffiliated" can fully communicate. Religious impulses, like the desire for connection and community, may be expressed in political activism. Sensibilities, like care for those who are poor, find their outlet in volunteer work or school systems. The desire for purpose, which we understand as a religious desire, may come through the dignity of a hard day's work at an entry-level job.

Connection, community, care for others, and purpose could easily be called human values, or even humanistic principles. Springtide is not just interested in the fact that these desires exist but that they are often sought within systems. When those systems fail to support, encourage, or fulfill those desires, young people will seek out new spaces and new systems, and they will create new traditions.

Our data make this clear. We know that the religious lives of young people—the things they long for and belong to, the ways they discover meaning, construct identity, and connect to others—are complicated. Thinking of shifts in social, religious, and cultural landscapes, the impact of current events, and the role of individual behaviors, this complexity isn't surprising. But it can be hard to navigate.

To help them flourish—and to keep them from floundering in isolation, stress, or meaninglessness—**young people need trusted adults, now more than ever.**

And now, *more than ever*, trusted adults need an effective approach—one that responds to these shifting realities and offers tools and practices for taking action.

We offer this new approach, Relational Authority, as a response to the dynamics that are at work in the world and in the lives of young people. This approach recognizes that young people need to feel that they have a bond, that they are *cared about*, before they can be receptive to authorities—that is, to the people in their lives who positively impact, influence, and guide them. **People like you.**

Better bonds, earned trust, and lasting influence in your relationships with young people are built on the five dimensions of Relational Authority: listening, transparency, integrity, care, and expertise. Intentionally practicing Relational Authority is a commitment to listening, caring for, engaging, and guiding young people as they navigate some of life's biggest questions and concerns. **The result, for those who are committed and intentional in the practice, is invaluable: lasting impact in the lives of young people, built on shared experience and sympathetic expertise.**

Appendix: Research Methodology

Quantitative Research

Springtide Research Institute collects quantitative data through surveys and qualitative data through interviews. The quantitative data tell us *what* is happening. The qualitative data tell us *why* and *how* it's happening.

For the quantitative data in this report, we conducted six primary studies over the last year, beginning in September 2019. While the specific phenomenon of each study varied, all projects (with the exception of the Social Distance Study) contained a set of repeating, foundational questions to measure demographics, meaning and relationships, trust in people and institutions, loneliness and belonging, religious affiliation, and religious practices. We surveyed a nationally representative sample of 13-to-25-year-olds in the United States, totaling 10,516 participants. The sample was weighted for age, gender, race, and region to match the demographics of the country, and it produced a margin of error of +/- 3%. The age, gender, racial, and regional demographics of this sample are as follows:

Age	Valid Percent
13–17	32%
18–21	37%
22–25	31%
Total	**100%**

Gender	Valid Percent
Girl/Woman or Transgender Girl/Woman	52%
Boy/Man or Transgender Boy/Man	46%
Non-binary	2%
Total	**100%**

Race	Valid Percent
White	54%
Hispanic or Latino	13%
Black or African American	21%
American Indian or Alaska Native	1%
Asian	9%
Native Hawaiian / Pacific Islander	0.5%
Other	2%

Region	Valid Percent
Northeast	18%
Midwest	22%
South	37%
West	23%

Tables may not add up to exactly 100% due to rounding.

Qualitative Research

For the qualitative research, we conducted 165 in-depth interviews either in person, via telephone, or via video. Interviews focused on understanding the relationships that young people depend on when they are looking for belonging, making decisions about their future, developing their political lens, and establishing their value systems. Conversations were guided but open ended, allowing for as much direction as possible from the interviewee. Interviews were transcribed and then analyzed thematically.

Interviews and survey responses are confidential, and all names of research participants in this report are pseudonyms. For more information or to obtain the survey instrument or request access to the data sets, please contact us at *research@springtideresearch.org*.

Acknowledgments

Created by the publishing team of Springtide Research Institute.

Printed in the United States of America
#5930
ISBN 978-1-64121-140-6

Research Team

Josh Packard, PhD, Executive Director

Megan Bissell, MA, Head Researcher

Adrianna Smell, MA, Associate Researcher

Sean Zimmy, Associate Researcher

Writing Team

Ellen Koneck, MAR, Head Writer and Editor

Josh Packard, PhD, Executive Director

Maura Thompson Hagarty, PhD, Developmental Editor

Creative Design & Production Team

Steven Mino

Brooke Saron

Becky Gochanour

Marte Aboagye

Sigrid Lindholm

References

Page 23—General Social Survey (GSS) Data Explorer. Strength of Religious Affiliation. 2018.

Page 27—Cigna. "Cigna's U.S. Loneliness Index: Survey of 20,000 Americans Examining Behaviors Driving Loneliness in the United States." May 2018.

Page 28—Gallup, Inc. Confidence in Institutions polling. 2019.

Page 34—Pew Research Center. "Early Benchmarks Show 'Post-Millennials' on Track to Be Most Diverse, Best-Educated Generation Yet." November 15, 2018.

Photo Credits

(All photos appear on Unsplash unless otherwise indicated.)

Resources Listed throughout the Report

The resources referenced in numbered marginal notes throughout this report are listed here, as well as at *springtideresearch.org/thestate2020*.

1. **Page 14 — Read:** Read *Belonging: Reconnecting America's Loneliest Generation* and learn more about the findings and insights from that report.

2. **Page 16 — Watch:** Watch a short video of Dr. Josh Packard unpacking the emotional pain that loneliness causes.

3. **Page 21 — Watch:** Watch Dr. Josh Packard discuss inclusion in a Lunch & Learn video Ellen Koneck.

4. **Page 25 — Watch:** Watch Dr. Josh Packard talk with Dr. Eugene C. Roehlkepartain from Search Institute, Sarah Kapostasy from Out Youth, and the team from The Institute for Youth Ministry at Princeton Theological Seminary in the five-part video series *What to Say to Young People During COVID-19.*

5. **Page 26 — Read:** Read in our Voices of Young People blog, our interview with Keziah, 13, about a self-portrait she painted while social distancing.

6. **Page 26 — Listen:** Listen to Emilie, 26, in *The Voices of Young People Podcast*, talk about the desire for deep conversation.

7. **Page 27 — Watch:** Dr. Josh Packard unpack surprising features that play into the epidemic of loneliness.

8. **Page 30 — Read:** Read about resources for responding to racism in a post featuring suggestions compiled by members of the Springtide Research Advisory Board.

9. **Page 31 — Listen:** Listen to Abdimalik, 24, in *The Voices of Young People Podcast*, talk about his experience as a Black young man in the aftermath of George Floyd's death.

10. **Page 36 — Watch:** Watch Dr. Josh Packard discuss the complexities of young people's religious lives and why it's important to focus on behaviors, not just labels.

11. **Page 37 / Page 44 — Data:** Find breakdowns of our key findings by race, gender, and region at *springtideresearch.org/thestate2020.*

12. **Page 45 — Listen:** Listen to season 3 of *The Voices of Young People Podcast*, which features ten young people telling us, in their own words, about their religious lives, identities, practices, and beliefs.

13. **Page 61 — Watch:** Watch a short video of Dr. Josh Packard unpacking the relationship between authority, titles, and trust.

14. **Page 63 — Watch:** Watch a short video of Dr. Josh Packard unpacking how to be a trusted guide—and why that's a big deal.

15. **Page 67 — Watch:** Watch a short video of Dr. Josh Packard present a webinar on the importance of relational ministry.

16. **Page 68 — Listen:** Listen to Jana, 21, in *The Voices of Young People Podcast*, talk about trusted adults.

17. **Page 74 — Watch:** Watch Dr. Josh Packard explaining the need to build trust with young people *and* their families.

18. **Page 80 — Read:** Read *Meaning Making: 8 Values That Drive America's Newest Generations*, and check out the additional free resources created to dive deeper.

19. **Page 82 — Watch:** Watch a short video of Dr. Josh Packard discussing care.

20. **Page 87 — Listen:** Listen to Jana, 21, in *The Voices of Young People Podcast*, talk about meaningful relationships.

21. **Page 94 — Watch:** Watch a short video of Dr. Josh Packard explaining the difference between isolation and choosing to be alone.

22. **Page 98 — Listen:** Listen to "Panorama for Orchestra," created by Conner, 23. He composed this piece in response to the question "How are you finding connection and meaning in these days of physical distancing?" Read our interview with him in our Voices of Young People blog.

23. **Page 105 — Watch:** Watch a Lunch & Learn video with Dr. Josh Packard and Ellen Koneck discussing what attracts young people to organizations.

Stay in Touch

Visit the Springtide website for a variety of resources to help you serve and support the young people in your life, including podcasts, blogs, video series, and our other reports and books. Find these resources and sign up for our biweekly newsletter at *springtideresearch.org*.

Join the conversation, and connect with us on social media.

Follow @WeAreSpringtide and use the hashtag #religionandyoungpeople2020 on Facebook, Instagram, and Twitter.

Share how you're building relationships amid complexity or practicing Relational Authority with the young people in your circle of care.
Send us a note at *stories@springtideresearch.org*.

Leaders like you are asking . . .

How do I know if my program is having the impact I want it to have?

What is going on in the lives of young people?

How can I position my organization for the future?

What isn't working in my organization, and how do I change it?

Let our expertise and experience fuel your passions, projects, and programs.

Our research services—including program evaluation, grant support, custom surveys, and more—combine this expertise with years of experience in applied research design, delivering actionable insights, so that you can focus on what matters: caring for young people better.

Learn more at *springtideresearch.org/services*

Notes:

Notes:

The free digital distribution of this report was made possible by a generous gift from an anonymous donor. We are deeply grateful for their partnership and support.

———————

Are you interested in supporting future publications?

For more information, contact Jessica Tomaselli, Director of Donor & Foundation Relations, at *jessica@springtideresearch.org*